■SCHOLASTIC

MW00352486

Ask & Answer
Interactive
Math Practice

240 Game Cards That Engage Students as They Read and Solve Math Problems and Build Essential Skills

by Joseph A. Porzio

New York • Toronto • London • Auckland • Sydney
Mexico City • New Delhi • Hong Kong • Buenos Aires

Teaching
Resources

Editor: Maria L. Chang
Cover design by Maria Lilja
Interior design by Kelli Thompson, Norma Ortiz

ISBN-13: 978-0-439-57213-2
ISBN-10: 0-439-57213-4
Copyright © 2007 by Joseph A. Porzio
Printed in the USA.

2 3 4 5 6 7 8 9 10 40   15 14 13 12 11 10 09 08

Table of Contents

Introduction

For more than 25 years, I have been conducting professional development sessions in mathematics for teachers, math coaches, and curriculum supervisors. At the beginning of these sessions, I often ask participants to list two or three major concerns they have regarding their work as math educators and leaders in their regions, districts, and schools. Over the years, I have collected, analyzed, and addressed thousands of these concerns, and it amazes me that *the concerns are always the same!* So much so, that it has become predictable which concepts, topics, and skills will appear on each new list. The following are a mere sampling of expressed concerns that are constants:

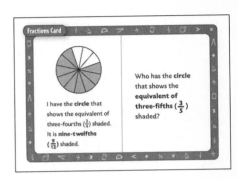

- *How can I teach the prescribed content and process strands at my grade level when my students are not ready for them?*

- *My students do not have mastery of their basic facts!*

- *Measurement skills are a major concern, especially in the area of metrics.*

- *Mathematical language necessary to communicate is often an area of need.*

- *Problem-solving skills are not an integral component of a student's background, e.g., make a model, draw a picture, look for a pattern, make a simpler problem, guess and check, etc.*

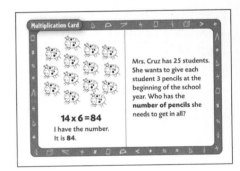

- *Students need to develop facility in recognizing the relatedness between/among fractions, decimals, and percents.*

The expressed concerns of math leaders and classroom teachers that I have collected over the years have led me to create activities designed to support foundation builders—early childhood and elementary-level classroom teachers—in their efforts to help their students master concepts and their related skills.

The activities in *Ask & Answer Interactive Math Practice* were not developed or intended to *teach* concepts related to multiplication, division, measurement, and other mathematical skills. Rather, they were designed to serve as a means to *reinforce and strengthen* basic skills with automaticity and accuracy while promoting communication and developing mathematical language.

Several years ago, the National Reading Panel issued a report titled "Teaching Children to Read—An Evidence-Based Assessment of the Scientific Research on Reading and Its Implications for Reading Instruction." One of the key areas addressed in the study is *fluency*, which is "generally acknowledged as a critical component of skilled reading." (See National Reading Panel, 3–1.) While the parallel may not be direct, it is my hope that the activities in this book will promote and support a fluency in mathematics that leads students to acquire mastery of concepts and automaticity (speed) and accuracy with regard to their related skills.

How to Use This Book

Inside, you'll find six sets of *Ask & Answer Interactive Math Practice* cards—a set each for reviewing basic concepts in multiplication; division; fractions; fractions, decimals & percents; geometry & measurement; and time. Each set consists of 40 cards with two sides: the left side features the *Answer* part, while the right side is the *Ask* part. The first student (or you, the teacher) starts by reading aloud the left side of the first card, then asking the question on the right side. Students have to listen carefully and pay close attention to see whether the left side of their card contains the answer to the question being posed. If it does, the student with the matching card reads aloud the answer then asks the next question. This cycle of asking and answering continues until the last card is read.

To facilitate this interactive review, start by making two photocopies of each complete set of cards. Keep one set intact. This will be your script to help you keep track of the correct order of cards. Cut apart the other set, making sure that each card has both sides. Each student should have at least one card. Whenever possible, provide students with more than one card, but make sure that an individual student's cards are *not* in sequence, so that a student doesn't answer his or her own question. NOTE: To ensure that every student can participate successfully, you may want to review each card and distribute the cards to individual students based upon their level of mastery of a topic.

Encourage students to study their cards and anticipate what question might be asked that would fit the answer that they have. As students develop confidence, understanding, and mastery, they can be given more-challenging cards.

At the onset of the activity, students will recognize the need to be attentive if they are to hear their

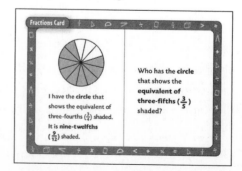

classmates ask, "*Who has…?*" As students gain understanding and confidence in the process involved in this activity, you may elect to have students respond in a more efficient manner, for example, not repeating what has been asked or simply stating the basic fact and its answer.

You may also want to make copies of several cards for display on an overhead projector. This will help students become familiar with the graphics, representations, and pictures that they might encounter in the texts and on state examinations. Representation is a key process strand found in the NCTM's *Principles and Standards for School Mathematics*. It promotes the use of representation to communicate mathematical ideas; translate representations to solve problems; and use representation to interpret physical, social, and mathematical phenomena. The challenges posed on the cards contain graphics (representations) that can be used to fulfill the key points found in the process strand.

You can also use the individual cards as the basis for writing activities. Invite students to write their own individual and/or small-group response to a card on their desk or one projected on a screen. Later, they can work cooperatively and collaboratively to create a series of topic-related questions that parallels the *Ask & Answer Interactive Math Practice* format.

— **Joseph A. Porzio**

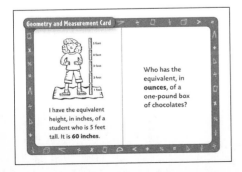

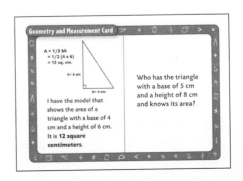

Connections to the NCTM Standards

Standard	Multiplication	Division	Fractions	Fractions Decimals & Percents	Geometry & Measurement	Time
Number and Numeration	●	●	●	●	●	●
Algebra						
Geometry			●	●	●	
Measurement			●	●	●	●
Data Analysis and Probability						
Problem Solving	●	●	●	●	●	●
Reasoning and Proof			●	●	●	●
Communication	●	●	●	●	●	●
Connections				●	●	●
Representation	●	●	●	●	●	●

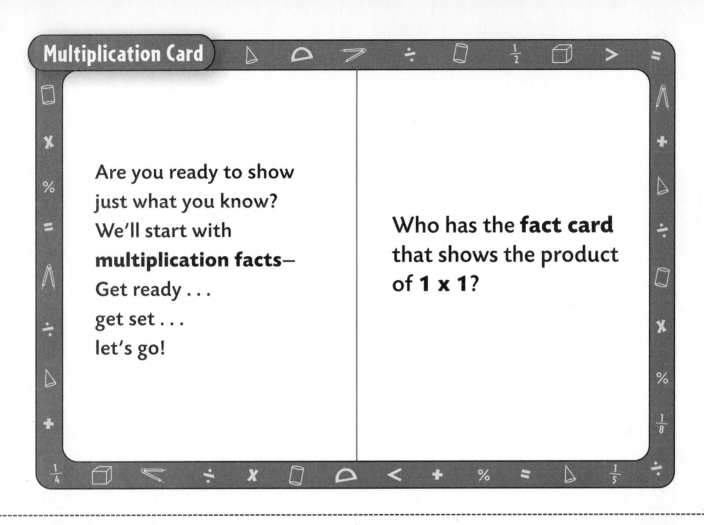

Multiplication Card

Are you ready to show just what you know? We'll start with **multiplication facts**—
Get ready . . .
get set . . .
let's go!

Who has the **fact card** that shows the product of **1 x 1**?

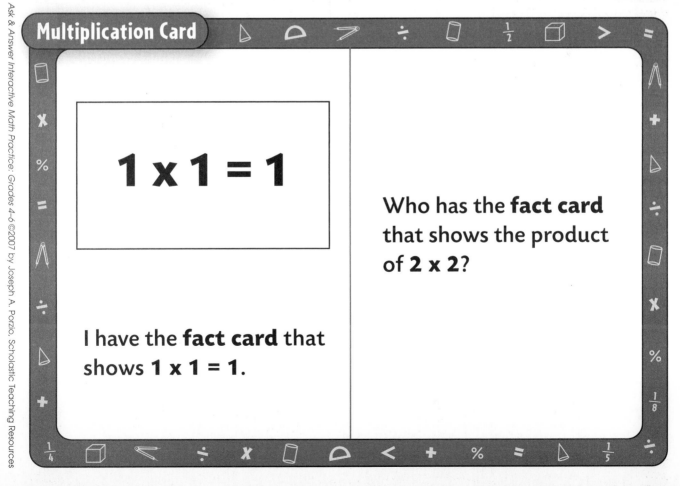

Multiplication Card

1 x 1 = 1

Who has the **fact card** that shows the product of **2 x 2**?

I have the **fact card** that shows **1 x 1 = 1**.

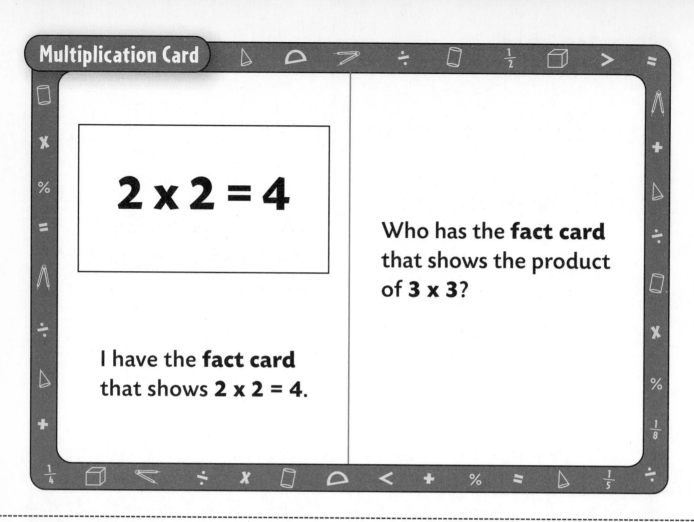

Multiplication Card

$2 \times 2 = 4$

Who has the **fact card** that shows the product of **3 x 3**?

I have the **fact card** that shows **2 x 2 = 4**.

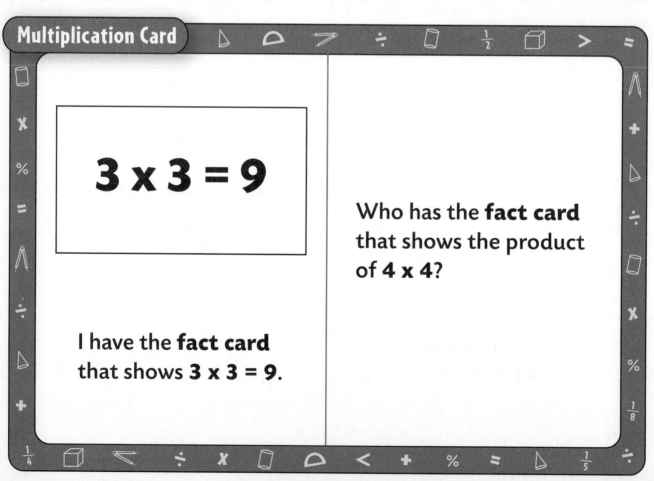

Multiplication Card

$3 \times 3 = 9$

Who has the **fact card** that shows the product of **4 x 4**?

I have the **fact card** that shows **3 x 3 = 9**.

Ask & Answer Interactive Math Practice: Grades 4–6 ©2007 by Joseph A. Porzio, Scholastic Teaching Resources

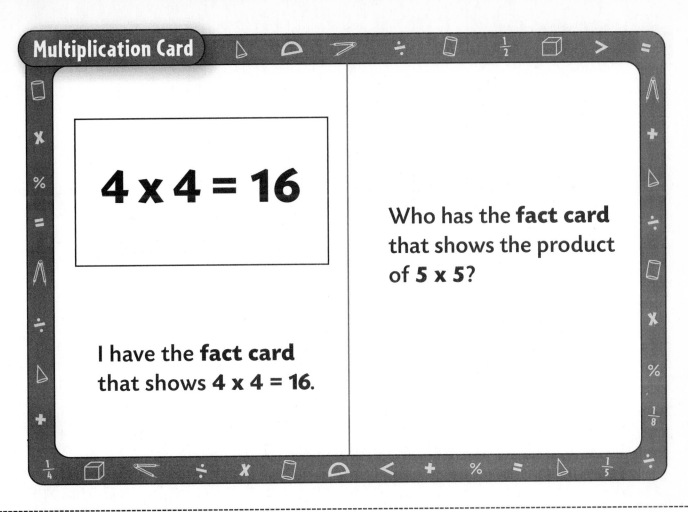

Multiplication Card

4 x 4 = 16

Who has the **fact card** that shows the product of **5 x 5**?

I have the **fact card** that shows **4 x 4 = 16**.

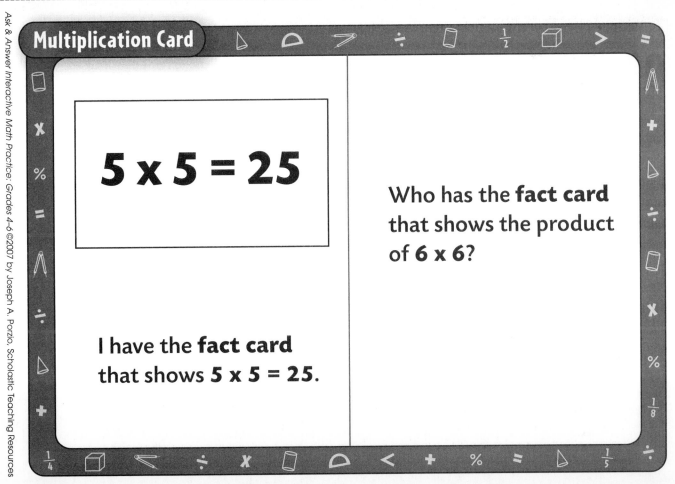

Multiplication Card

5 x 5 = 25

Who has the **fact card** that shows the product of **6 x 6**?

I have the **fact card** that shows **5 x 5 = 25**.

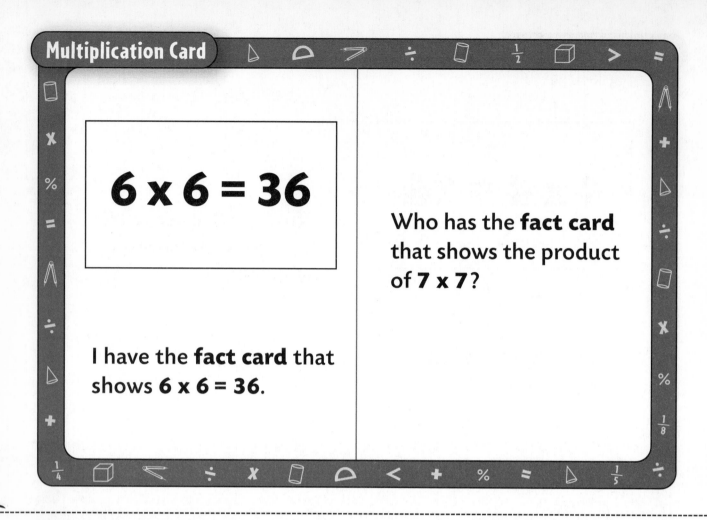

Multiplication Card

$6 \times 6 = 36$

Who has the **fact card** that shows the product of **7 x 7**?

I have the **fact card** that shows **6 x 6 = 36**.

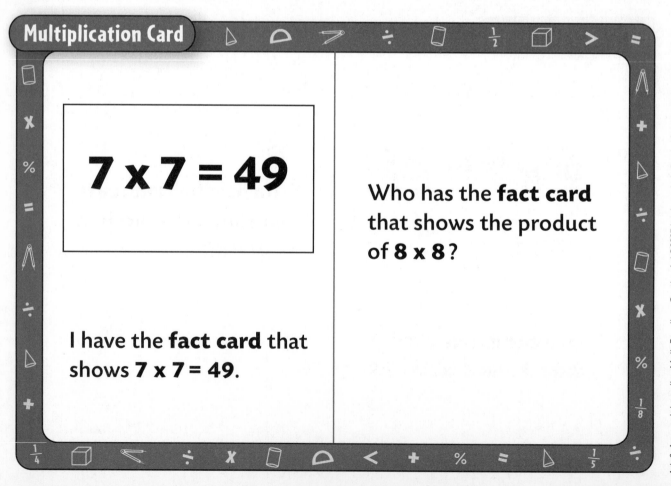

Multiplication Card

$7 \times 7 = 49$

Who has the **fact card** that shows the product of **8 x 8**?

I have the **fact card** that shows **7 x 7 = 49**.

Ask & Answer Interactive Math Practice: Grades 4–6 ©2007 by Joseph A. Porzio, Scholastic Teaching Resources

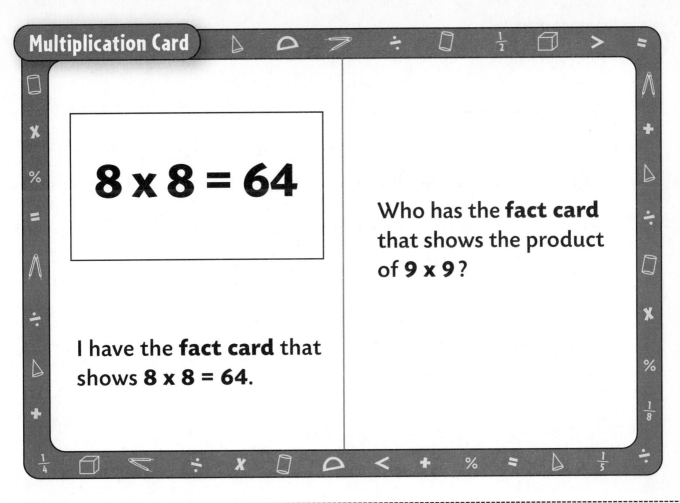

Multiplication Card

$$8 \times 8 = 64$$

Who has the **fact card** that shows the product of **9 x 9**?

I have the **fact card** that shows **8 x 8 = 64**.

$\frac{1}{4}$

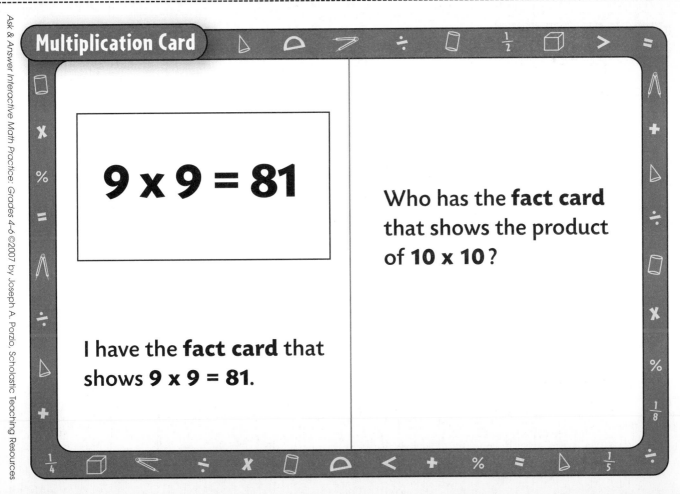

Multiplication Card

$$9 \times 9 = 81$$

Who has the **fact card** that shows the product of **10 x 10**?

I have the **fact card** that shows **9 x 9 = 81**.

$\frac{1}{4}$

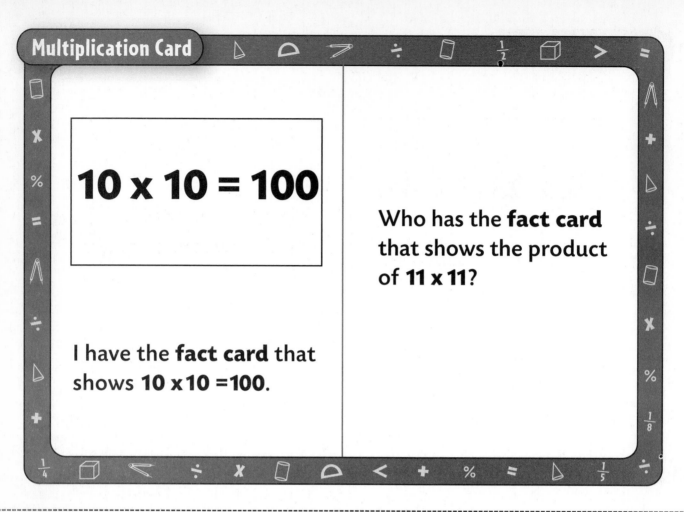

Multiplication Card

10 x 10 = 100

Who has the **fact card** that shows the product of **11 x 11**?

I have the **fact card** that shows **10 x 10 = 100**.

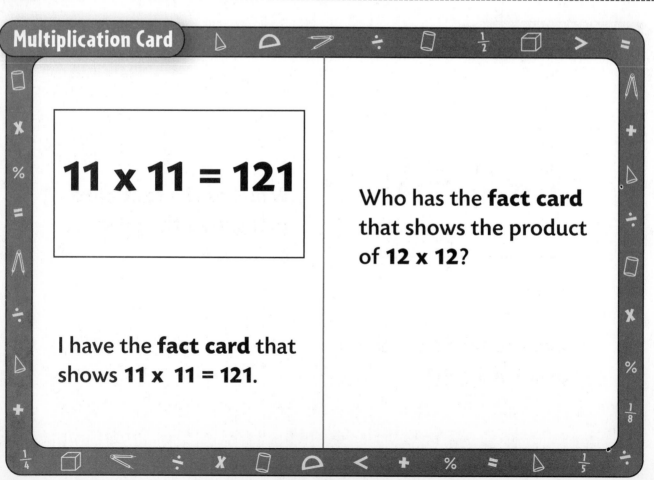

Multiplication Card

11 x 11 = 121

Who has the **fact card** that shows the product of **12 x 12**?

I have the **fact card** that shows **11 x 11 = 121**.

Ask & Answer Interactive Math Practice: Grades 4–6 ©2007 by Joseph A. Porzio, Scholastic Teaching Resources

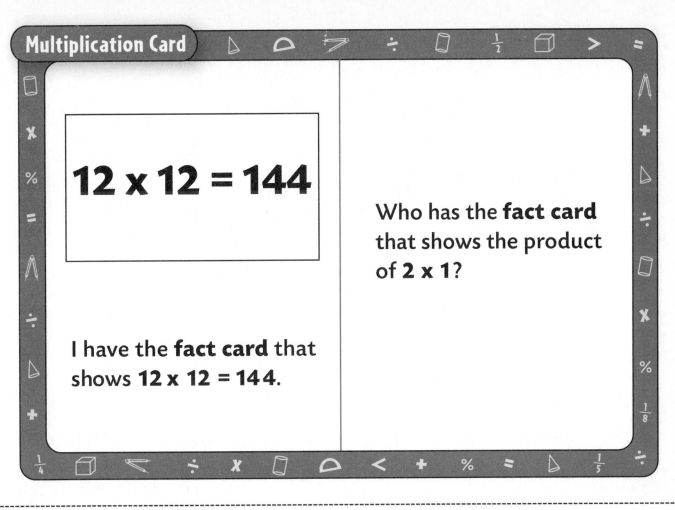

Multiplication Card

$$12 \times 12 = 144$$

Who has the **fact card** that shows the product of **2 x 1**?

I have the **fact card** that shows **12 x 12 = 144**.

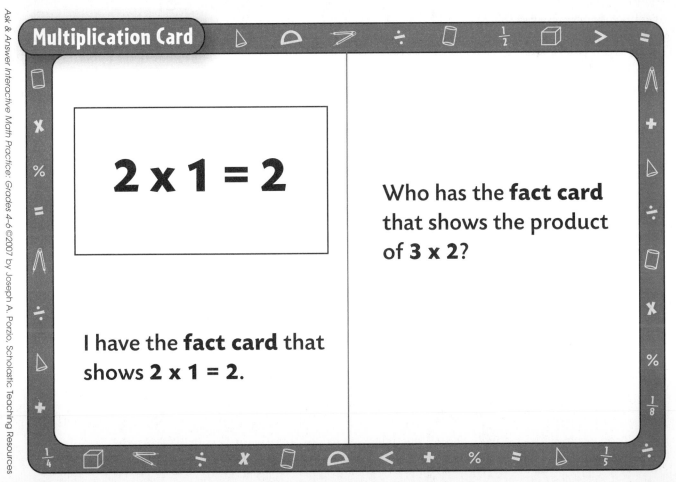

Multiplication Card

$$2 \times 1 = 2$$

Who has the **fact card** that shows the product of **3 x 2**?

I have the **fact card** that shows **2 x 1 = 2**.

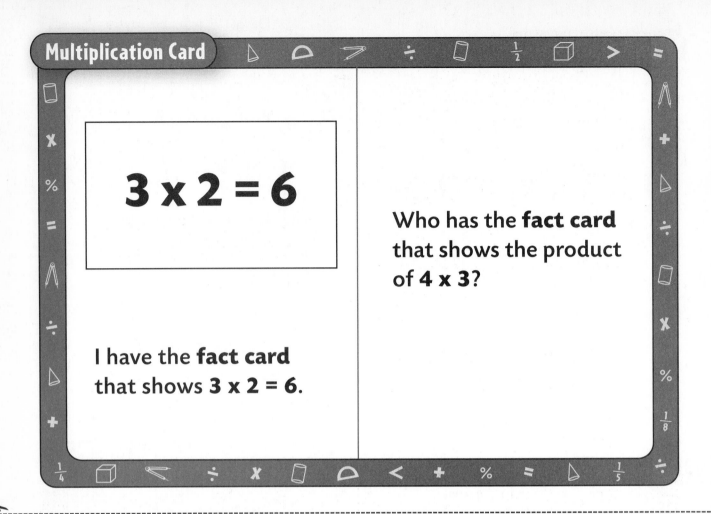

$$3 \times 2 = 6$$

Who has the **fact card** that shows the product of **4 x 3**?

I have the **fact card** that shows **3 x 2 = 6**.

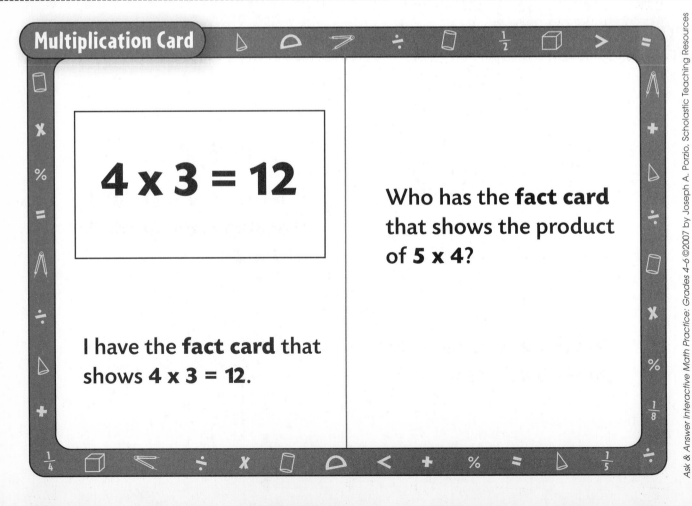

$$4 \times 3 = 12$$

Who has the **fact card** that shows the product of **5 x 4**?

I have the **fact card** that shows **4 x 3 = 12**.

Ask & Answer Interactive Math Practice: Grades 4–6 ©2007 by Joseph A. Porzio, Scholastic Teaching Resources

Ask & Answer Interactive Math Practice: Grades 4–6 ©2007 by Joseph A. Porzio, Scholastic Teaching Resources

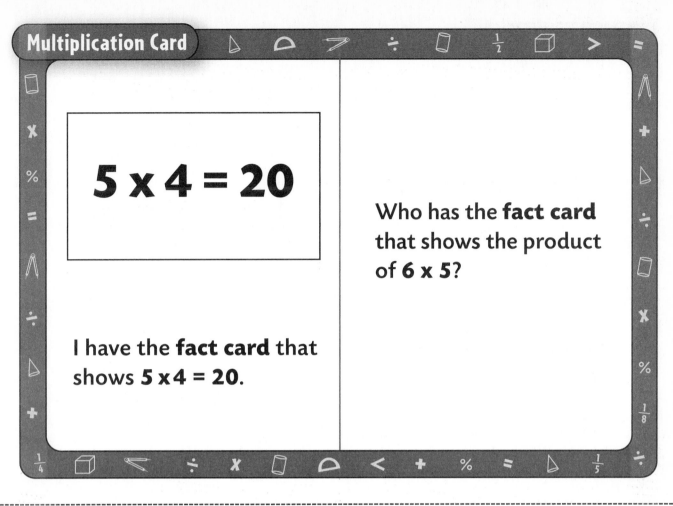

Multiplication Card

$$5 \times 4 = 20$$

Who has the **fact card** that shows the product of **6 x 5**?

I have the **fact card** that shows **5 x 4 = 20**.

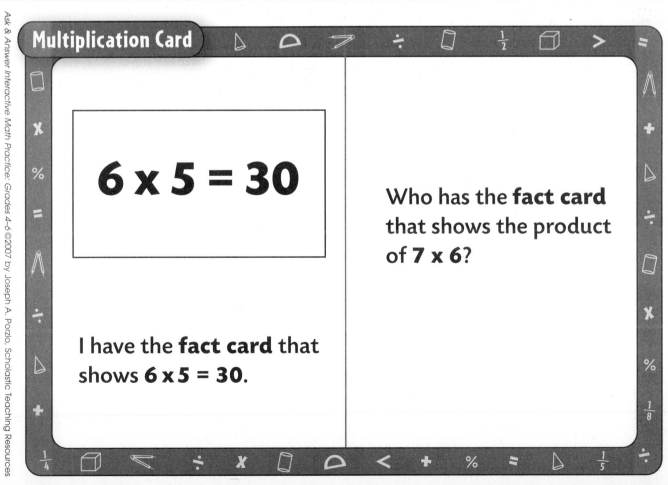

Multiplication Card

$$6 \times 5 = 30$$

Who has the **fact card** that shows the product of **7 x 6**?

I have the **fact card** that shows **6 x 5 = 30**.

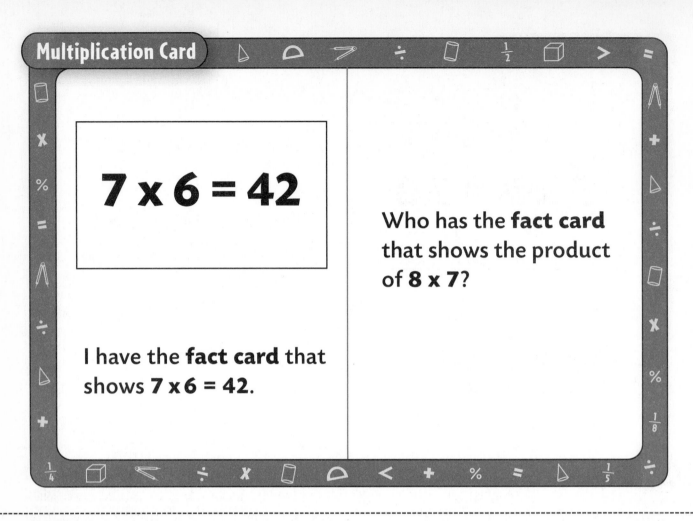

Multiplication Card

7 x 6 = 42

Who has the **fact card** that shows the product of **8 x 7**?

I have the **fact card** that shows **7 x 6 = 42**.

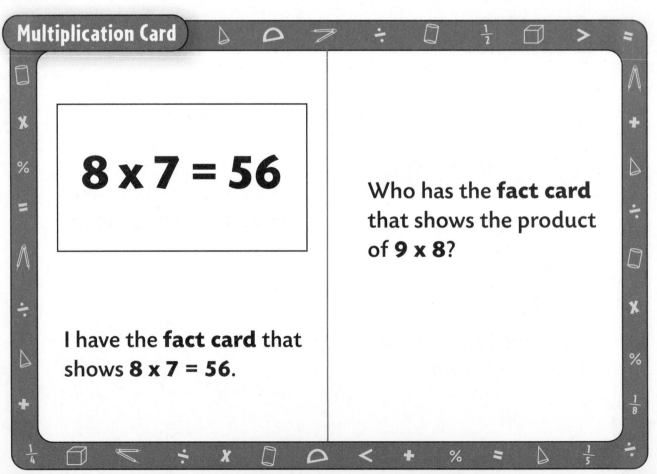

Multiplication Card

8 x 7 = 56

Who has the **fact card** that shows the product of **9 x 8**?

I have the **fact card** that shows **8 x 7 = 56**.

Ask & Answer Interactive Math Practice: Grades 4–6 ©2007 by Joseph A. Porzio, Scholastic Teaching Resources

Ask & Answer Interactive Math Practice: Grades 4–6 ©2007 by Joseph A. Porzio. Scholastic Teaching Resources

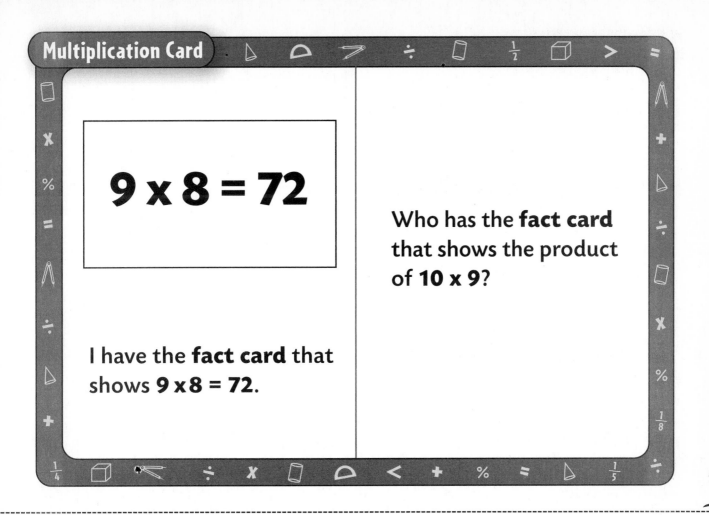

Multiplication Card

$$9 \times 8 = 72$$

Who has the **fact card** that shows the product of **10 x 9**?

I have the **fact card** that shows **9 x 8 = 72**.

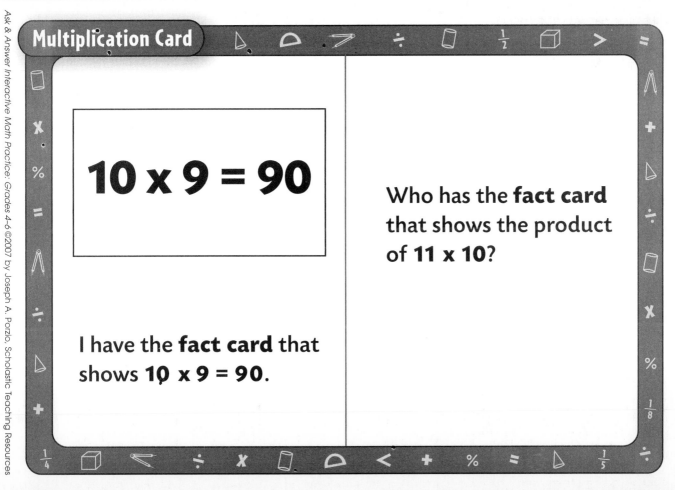

Multiplication Card

$$10 \times 9 = 90$$

Who has the **fact card** that shows the product of **11 x 10**?

I have the **fact card** that shows **10 x 9 = 90**.

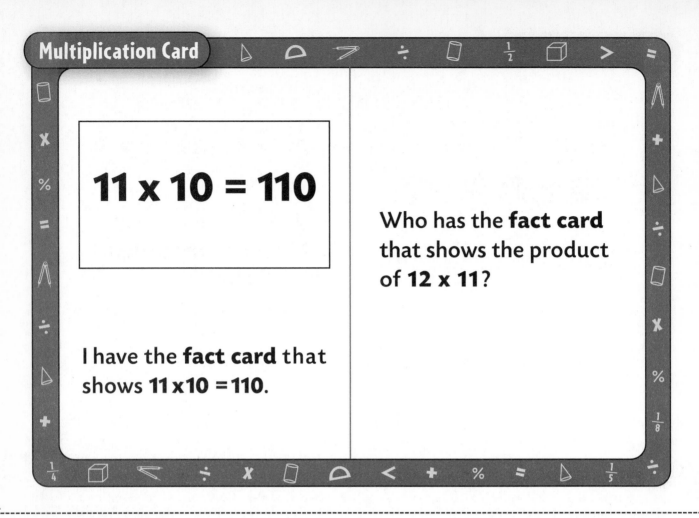

Multiplication Card

11 x 10 = 110

Who has the **fact card** that shows the product of **12 x 11**?

I have the **fact card** that shows **11 x 10 = 110**.

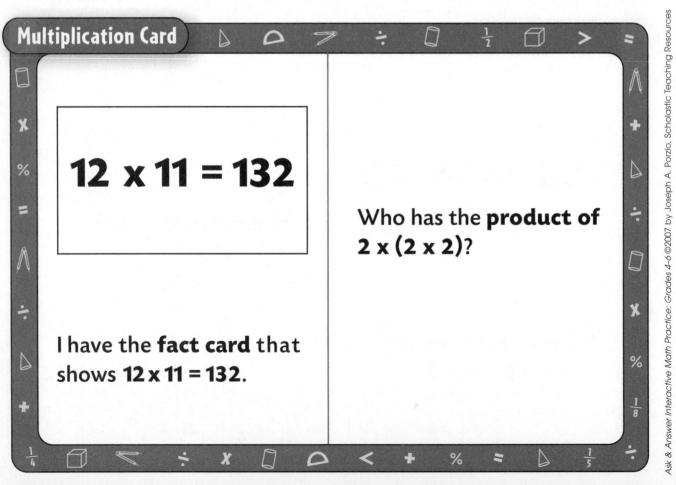

Multiplication Card

12 x 11 = 132

Who has the **product of 2 x (2 x 2)**?

I have the **fact card** that shows **12 x 11 = 132**.

Ask & Answer Interactive Math Practice: Grades 4–6 ©2007 by Joseph A. Porzio, Scholastic Teaching Resources

$$2 \times (2 \times 2) = 8$$

Who has the **product** of 2 x (3 x 2)?

I have the **product**. It is **8**.

$$2 \times (3 \times 2) = 12$$

Who has the **product** of 3 x (3 x 3)?

I have the **product**. It is **12**.

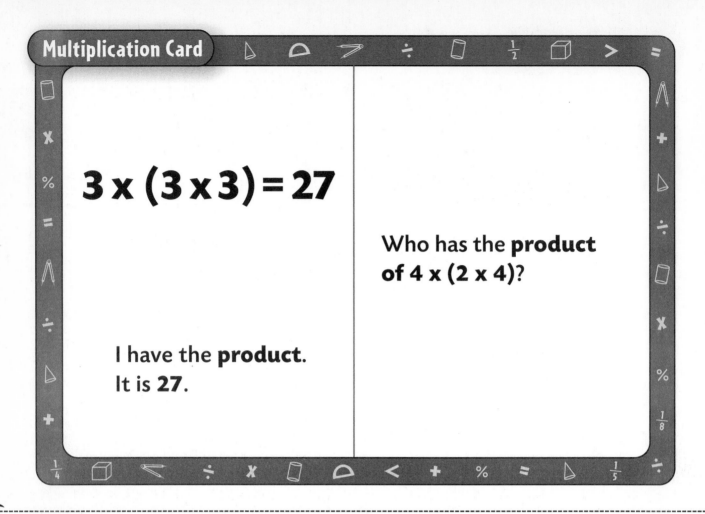

Multiplication Card

$$3 \times (3 \times 3) = 27$$

I have the **product**.
It is **27**.

Who has the **product of 4 x (2 x 4)**?

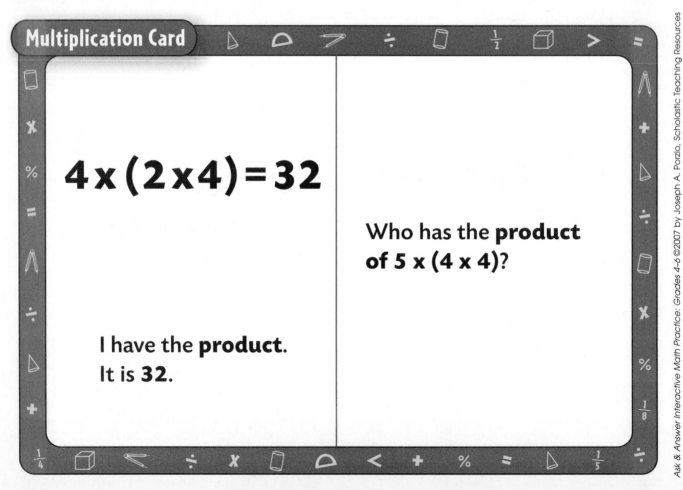

Multiplication Card

$$4 \times (2 \times 4) = 32$$

I have the **product**.
It is **32**.

Who has the **product of 5 x (4 x 4)**?

Ask & Answer Interactive Math Practice: Grades 4–6 ©2007 by Joseph A. Porzio, Scholastic Teaching Resources

Ask & Answer Interactive Math Practice: Grades 4–6 ©2007 by Joseph A. Porzio, Scholastic Teaching Resources

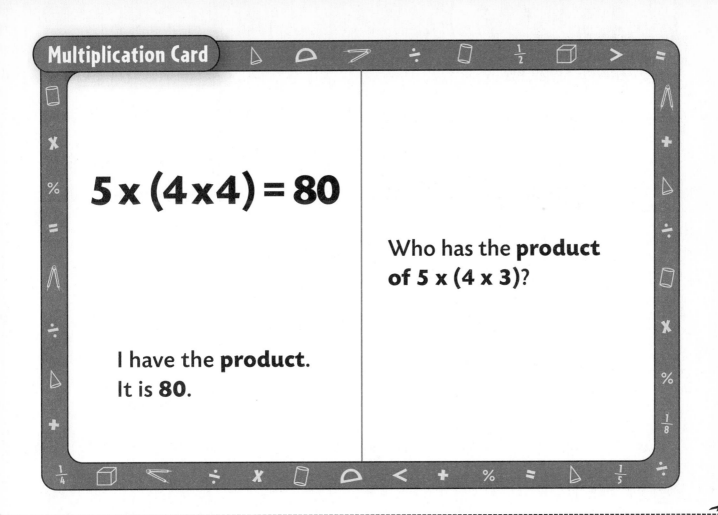

Multiplication Card

$$5 \times (4 \times 4) = 80$$

Who has the **product of 5 x (4 x 3)**?

I have the **product**. It is **80**.

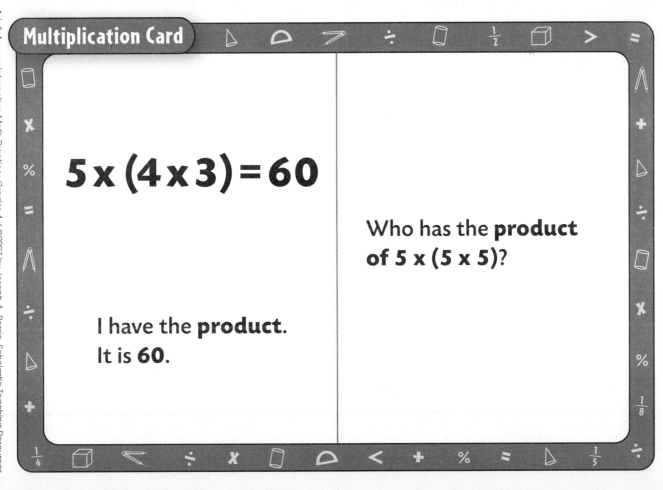

Multiplication Card

$$5 \times (4 \times 3) = 60$$

Who has the **product of 5 x (5 x 5)**?

I have the **product**. It is **60**.

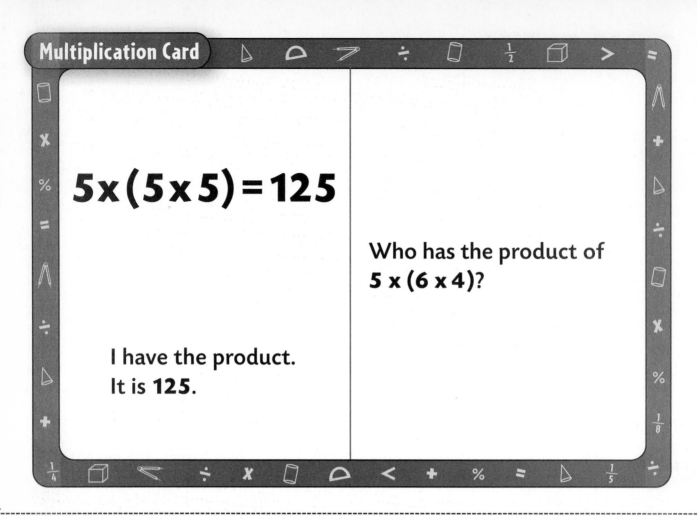

Multiplication Card

$$5 \times (5 \times 5) = 125$$

Who has the product of
5 x (6 x 4)?

I have the product.
It is **125**.

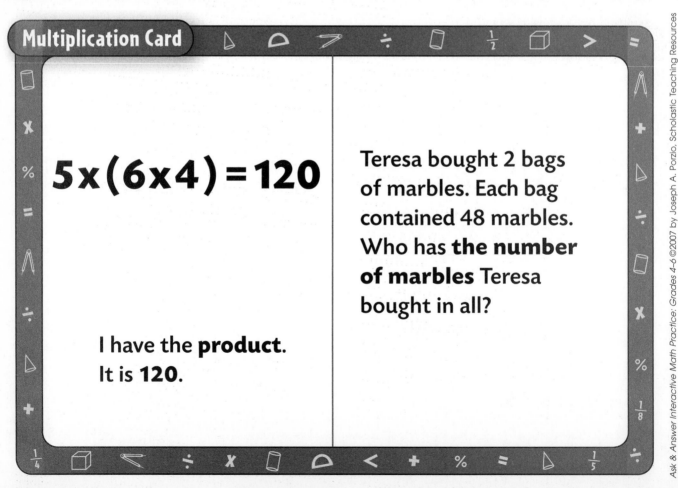

Multiplication Card

$$5 \times (6 \times 4) = 120$$

Teresa bought 2 bags
of marbles. Each bag
contained 48 marbles.
Who has **the number
of marbles** Teresa
bought in all?

I have the **product**.
It is **120**.

Ask & Answer Interactive Math Practice: Grades 4–6 ©2007 by Joseph A. Porzio. Scholastic Teaching Resources

Multiplication Card

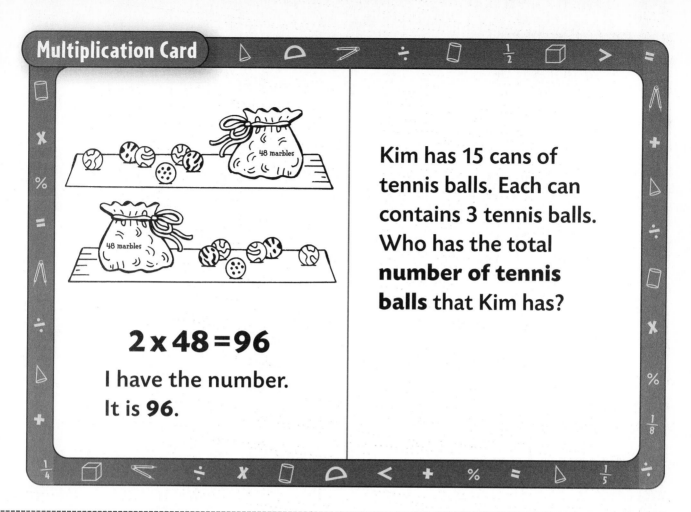

2 × 48 = 96

I have the number.
It is **96**.

Kim has 15 cans of tennis balls. Each can contains 3 tennis balls. Who has the total **number of tennis balls** that Kim has?

Multiplication Card

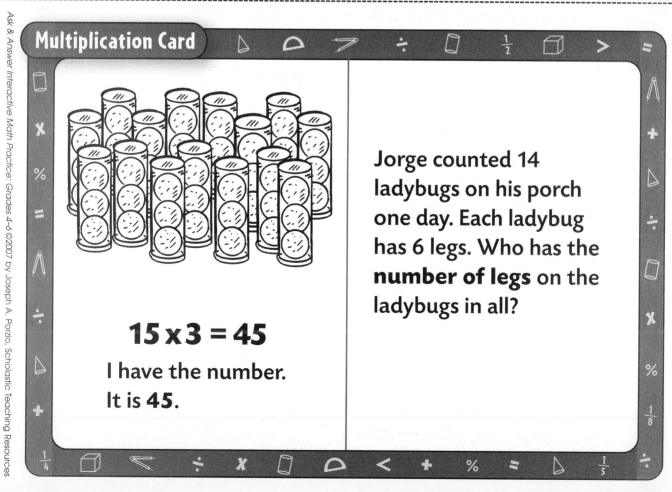

15 × 3 = 45

I have the number.
It is **45**.

Jorge counted 14 ladybugs on his porch one day. Each ladybug has 6 legs. Who has the **number of legs** on the ladybugs in all?

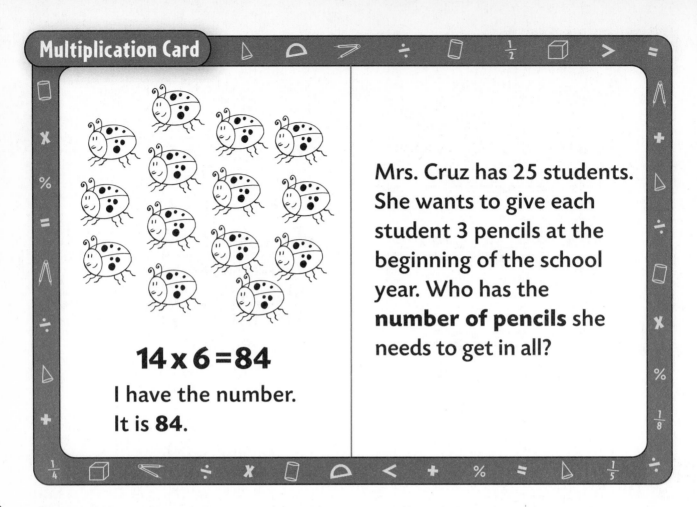

14 x 6 = 84

I have the number.
It is **84**.

Mrs. Cruz has 25 students. She wants to give each student 3 pencils at the beginning of the school year. Who has the **number of pencils** she needs to get in all?

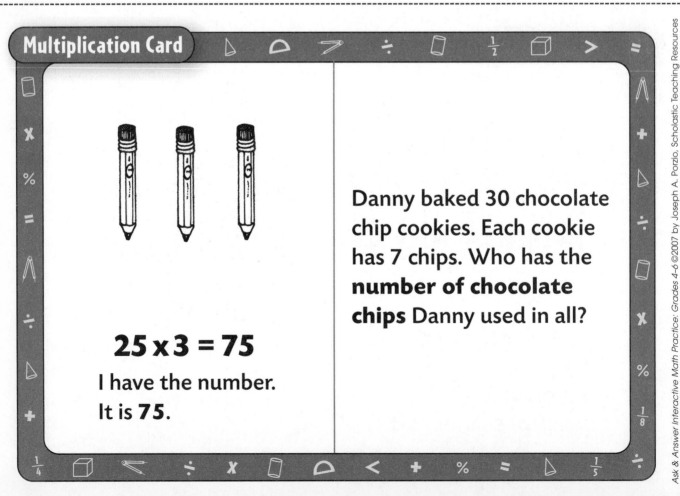

25 x 3 = 75

I have the number.
It is **75**.

Danny baked 30 chocolate chip cookies. Each cookie has 7 chips. Who has the **number of chocolate chips** Danny used in all?

Ask & Answer Interactive Math Practice: Grades 4–6 ©2007 by Joseph A. Porzio, Scholastic Teaching Resources

Multiplication Card

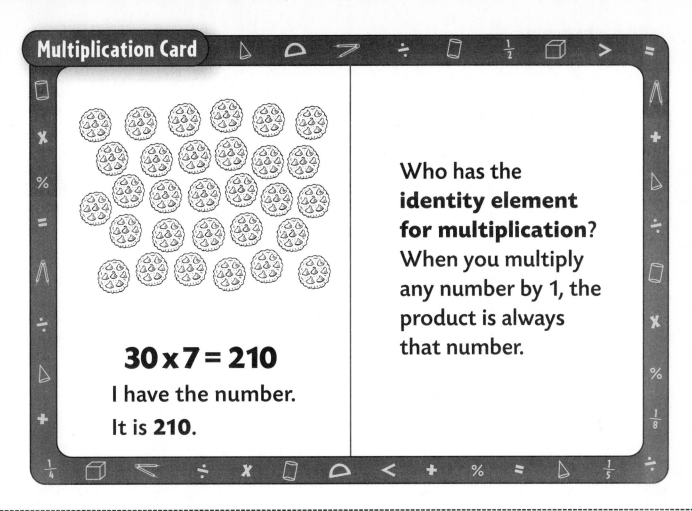

30 x 7 = 210

I have the number.
It is **210**.

Who has the
**identity element
for multiplication**?
When you multiply
any number by 1, the
product is always
that number.

Multiplication Card

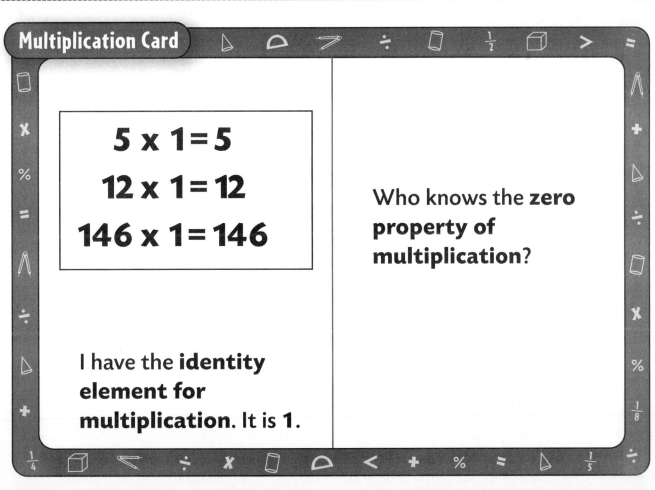

5 x 1 = 5
12 x 1 = 12
146 x 1 = 146

I have the **identity
element for
multiplication**. It is **1**.

Who knows the **zero
property of
multiplication**?

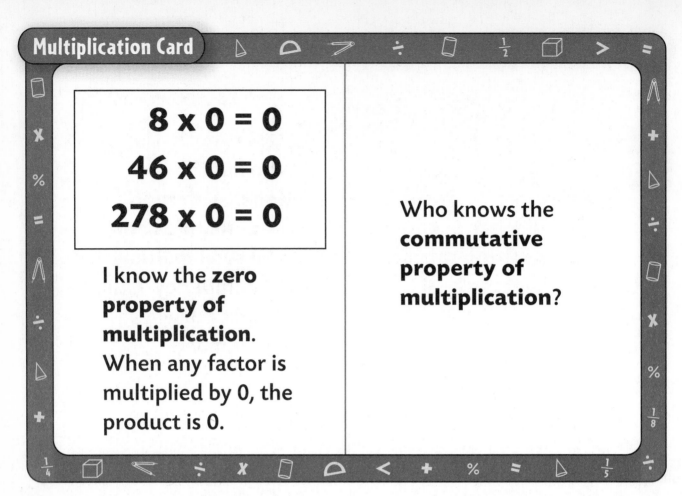

Multiplication Card

$$8 \times 0 = 0$$
$$46 \times 0 = 0$$
$$278 \times 0 = 0$$

I know the **zero property of multiplication.** When any factor is multiplied by 0, the product is 0.

Who knows the **commutative property of multiplication?**

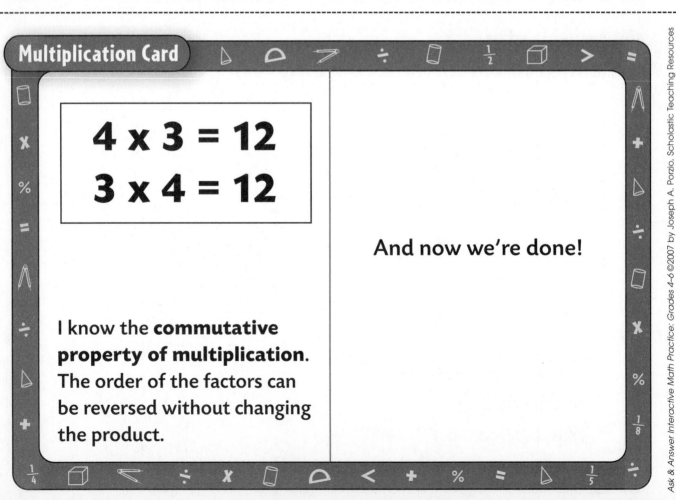

Multiplication Card

$$4 \times 3 = 12$$
$$3 \times 4 = 12$$

I know the **commutative property of multiplication.** The order of the factors can be reversed without changing the product.

And now we're done!

Ask & Answer Interactive Math Practice: Grades 4–6 ©2007 by Joseph A. Porzio, Scholastic Teaching Resources

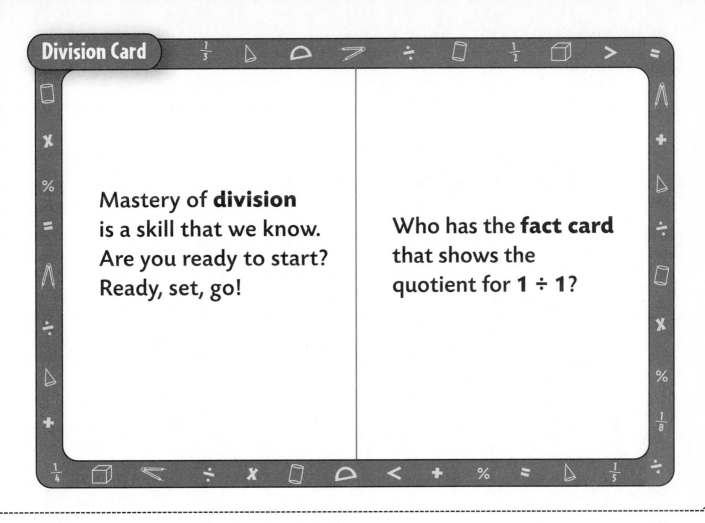

Division Card

Mastery of **division**
is a skill that we know.
Are you ready to start?
Ready, set, go!

Who has the **fact card**
that shows the
quotient for **1 ÷ 1**?

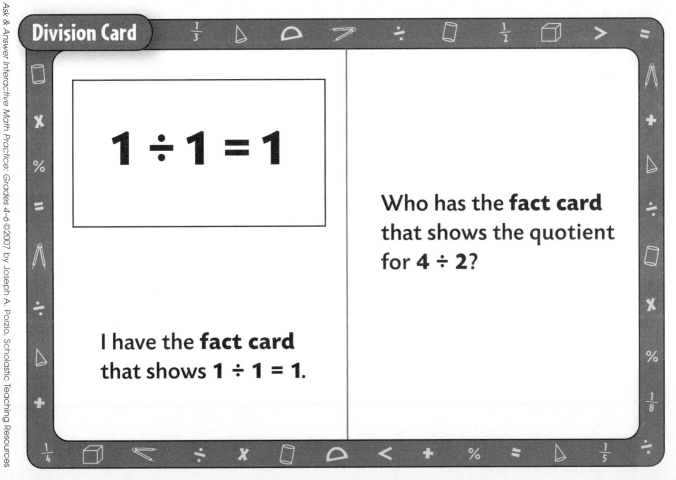

Division Card

1 ÷ 1 = 1

Who has the **fact card**
that shows the quotient
for **4 ÷ 2**?

I have the **fact card**
that shows **1 ÷ 1 = 1**.

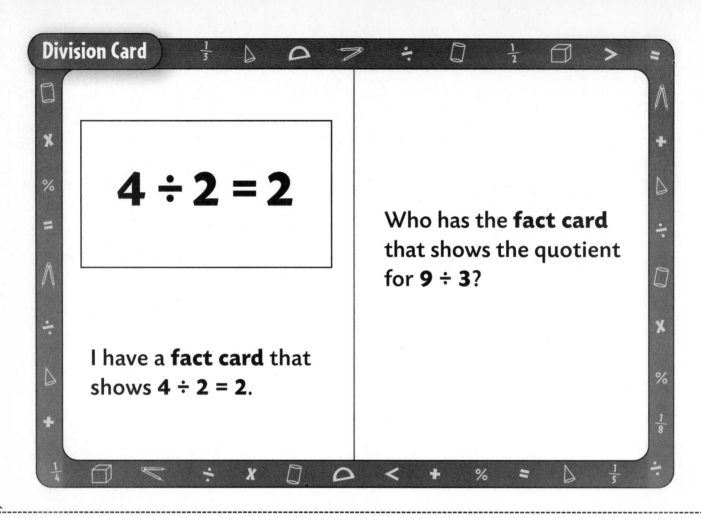

Division Card

$$4 \div 2 = 2$$

Who has the **fact card** that shows the quotient for **9 ÷ 3**?

I have a **fact card** that shows **4 ÷ 2 = 2**.

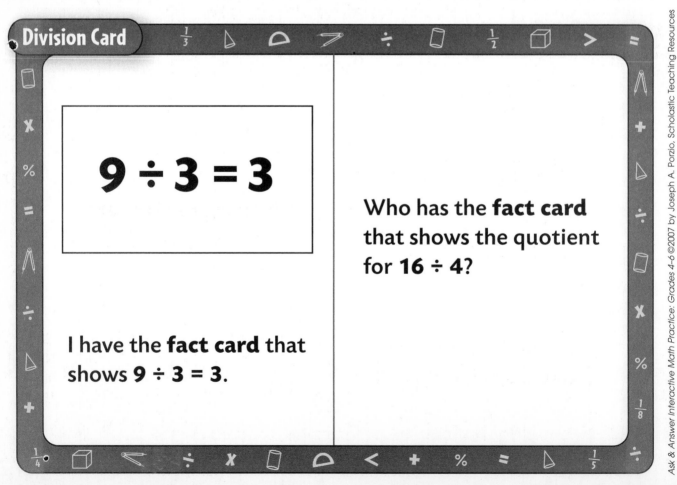

Division Card

$$9 \div 3 = 3$$

Who has the **fact card** that shows the quotient for **16 ÷ 4**?

I have the **fact card** that shows **9 ÷ 3 = 3**.

Ask & Answer Interactive Math Practice: Grades 4–6 ©2007 by Joseph A. Porzio, Scholastic Teaching Resources

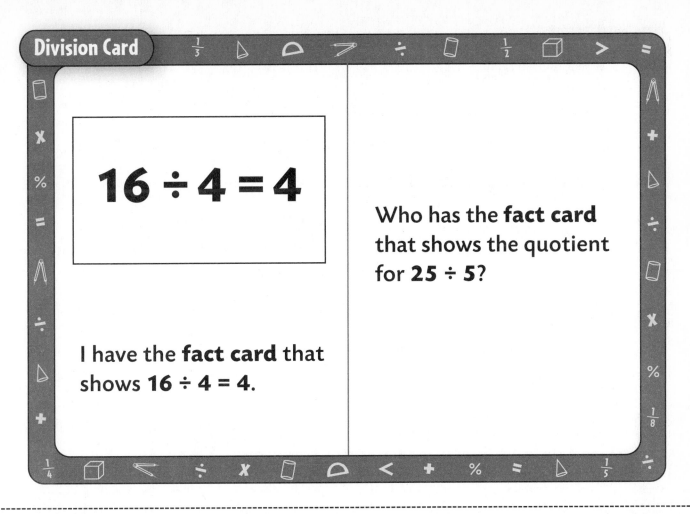

Division Card

$$16 \div 4 = 4$$

Who has the **fact card** that shows the quotient for **25 ÷ 5**?

I have the **fact card** that shows **16 ÷ 4 = 4**.

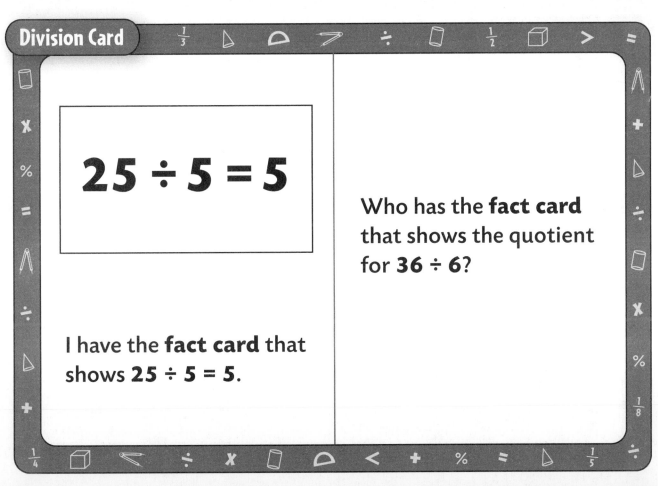

Division Card

$$25 \div 5 = 5$$

Who has the **fact card** that shows the quotient for **36 ÷ 6**?

I have the **fact card** that shows **25 ÷ 5 = 5**.

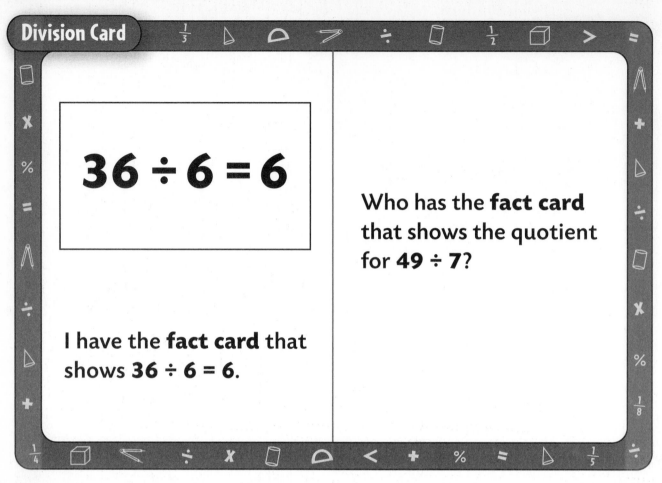

Division Card

$$36 \div 6 = 6$$

Who has the **fact card** that shows the quotient for **49 ÷ 7**?

I have the **fact card** that shows **36 ÷ 6 = 6**.

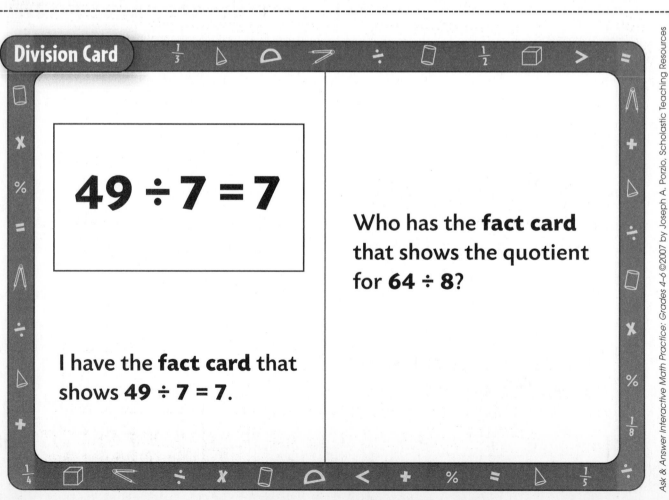

Division Card

$$49 \div 7 = 7$$

Who has the **fact card** that shows the quotient for **64 ÷ 8**?

I have the **fact card** that shows **49 ÷ 7 = 7**.

Ask & Answer Interactive Math Practice: Grades 4–6 ©2007 by Joseph A. Porzio, Scholastic Teaching Resources

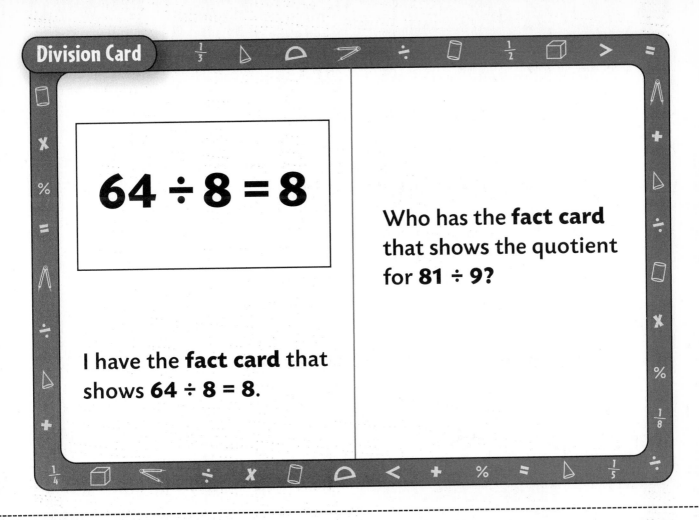

Division Card

$$64 \div 8 = 8$$

Who has the **fact card** that shows the quotient for **81 ÷ 9?**

I have the **fact card** that shows **64 ÷ 8 = 8**.

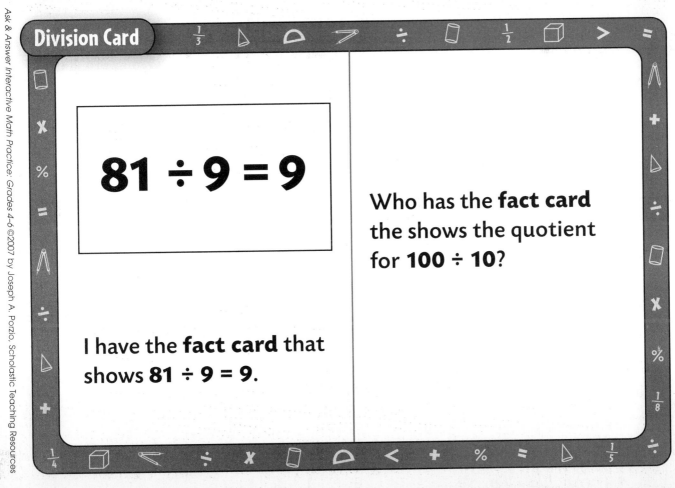

Division Card

$$81 \div 9 = 9$$

Who has the **fact card** the shows the quotient for **100 ÷ 10?**

I have the **fact card** that shows **81 ÷ 9 = 9**.

Ask & Answer Interactive Math Practice: Grades 4-6 ©2007 by Joseph A. Porzio, Scholastic Teaching Resources

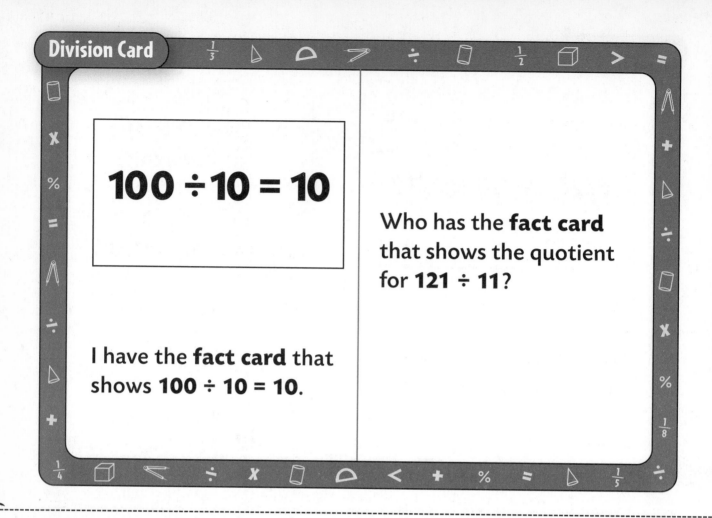

$$100 \div 10 = 10$$

Who has the **fact card** that shows the quotient for **121 ÷ 11**?

I have the **fact card** that shows **100 ÷ 10 = 10**.

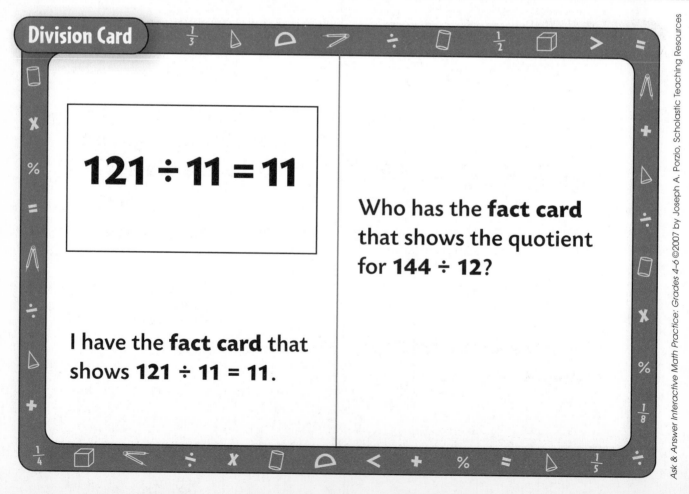

$$121 \div 11 = 11$$

Who has the **fact card** that shows the quotient for **144 ÷ 12**?

I have the **fact card** that shows **121 ÷ 11 = 11**.

Ask & Answer Interactive Math Practice: Grades 4–6 ©2007 by Joseph A. Porzio, Scholastic Teaching Resources

$144 \div 12 = 12$

When I divide 2 by this divisor, the quotient is 1. Who has the **divisor**?

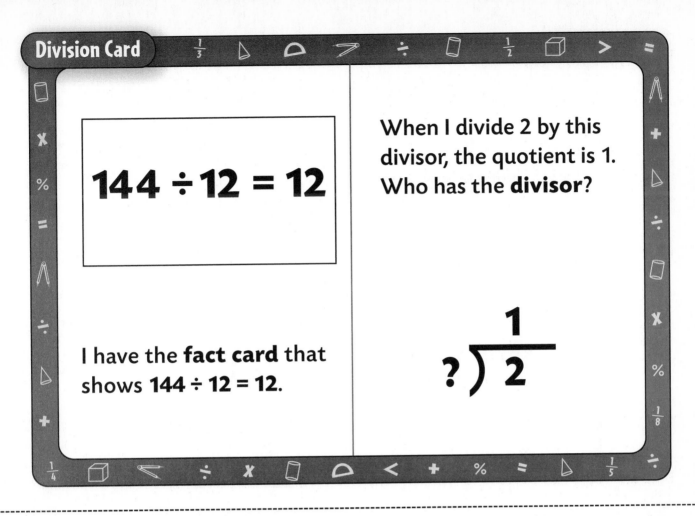

$? \overline{)\, 2}^{\,1}$

I have the **fact card** that shows **144 ÷ 12 = 12**.

Division Card

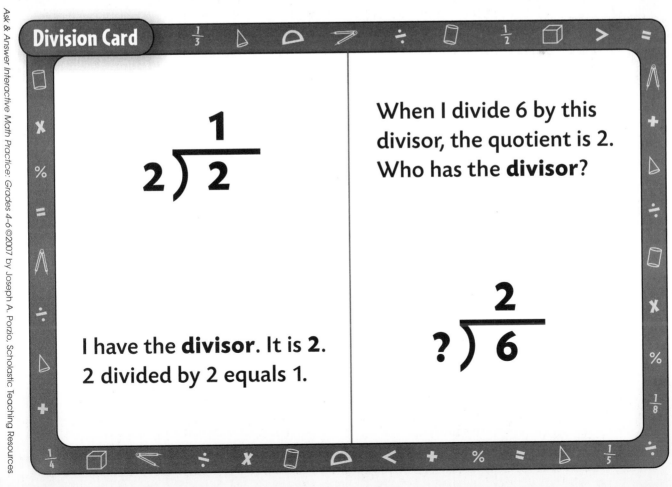

$2 \overline{)\, 2}^{\,1}$

When I divide 6 by this divisor, the quotient is 2. Who has the **divisor**?

$? \overline{)\, 6}^{\,2}$

I have the **divisor**. It is **2**. 2 divided by 2 equals 1.

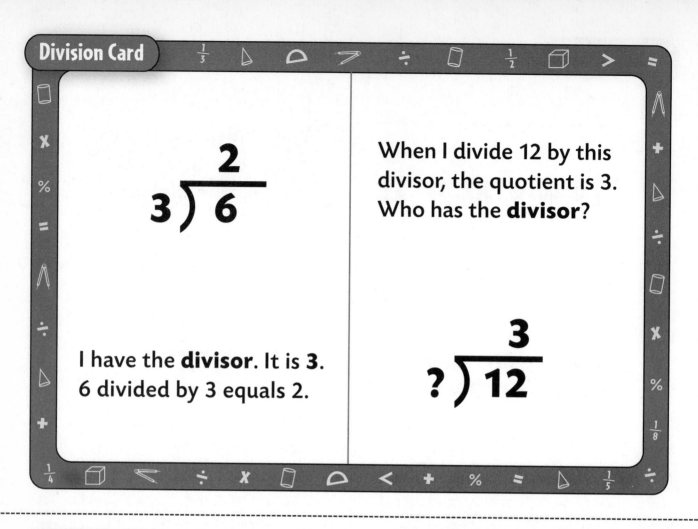

I have the **divisor**. It is **3**.
6 divided by 3 equals 2.

When I divide 12 by this divisor, the quotient is 3. Who has the **divisor**?

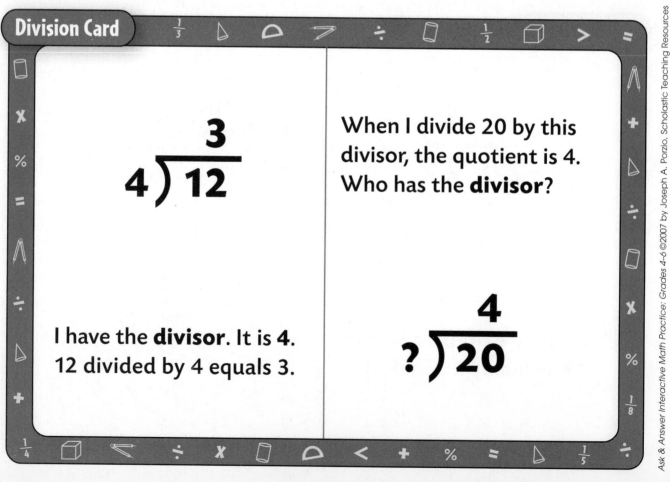

I have the **divisor**. It is **4**.
12 divided by 4 equals 3.

When I divide 20 by this divisor, the quotient is 4. Who has the **divisor**?

Ask & Answer Interactive Math Practice: Grades 4–6 ©2007 by Joseph A. Porzio, Scholastic Teaching Resources

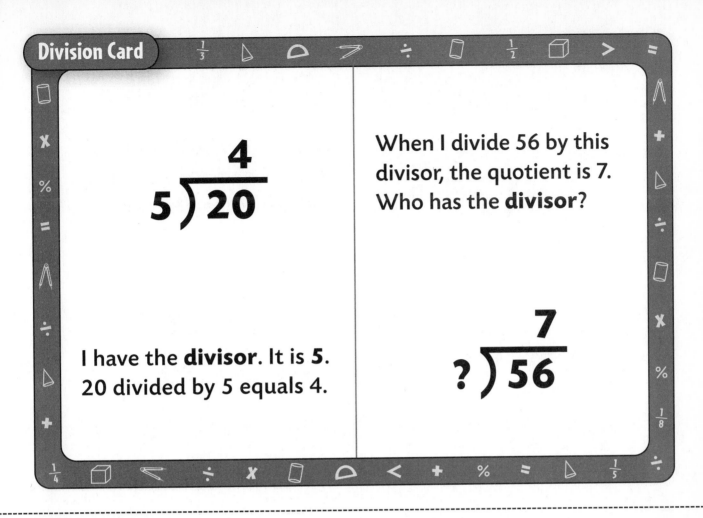

4
5)‾20‾

When I divide 56 by this divisor, the quotient is 7. Who has the **divisor**?

7
?)‾56‾

I have the **divisor**. It is **5**. 20 divided by 5 equals 4.

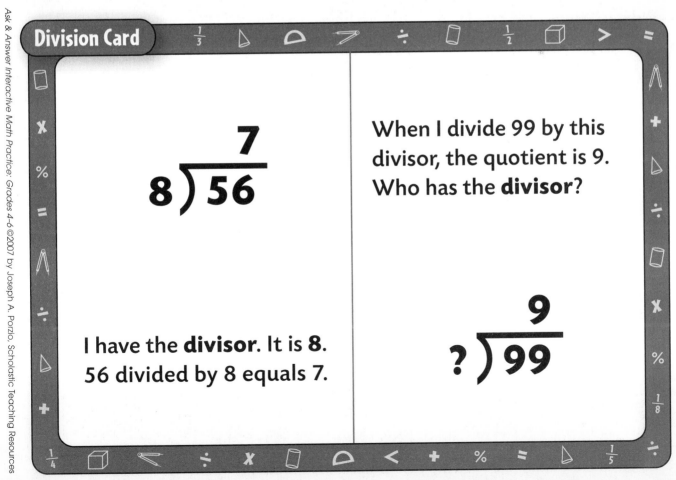

7
8)‾56‾

When I divide 99 by this divisor, the quotient is 9. Who has the **divisor**?

9
?)‾99‾

I have the **divisor**. It is **8**. 56 divided by 8 equals 7.

Ask & Answer Interactive Math Practice: Grades 4–6 ©2007 by Joseph A. Porzio, Scholastic Teaching Resources

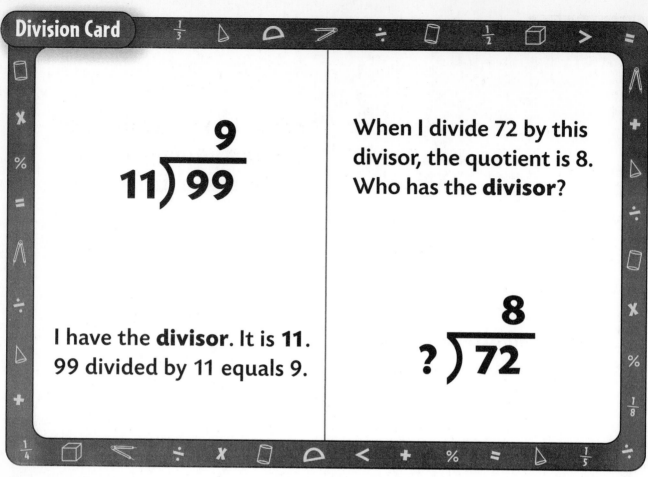

$11\overline{)99}^{\,9}$

When I divide 72 by this divisor, the quotient is 8. Who has the **divisor**?

I have the **divisor**. It is **11**. 99 divided by 11 equals 9.

$?\overline{)72}^{\,8}$

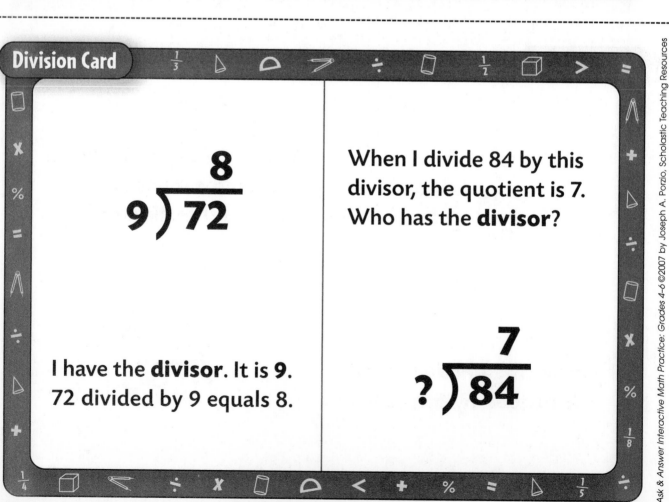

$9\overline{)72}^{\,8}$

When I divide 84 by this divisor, the quotient is 7. Who has the **divisor**?

I have the **divisor**. It is **9**. 72 divided by 9 equals 8.

$?\overline{)84}^{\,7}$

Ask & Answer Interactive Math Practice: Grades 4–6 ©2007 by Joseph A. Porzio, Scholastic Teaching Resources

Ask & Answer Interactive Math Practice: Grades 4–6 ©2007 by Joseph A. Porzio. Scholastic Teaching Resources

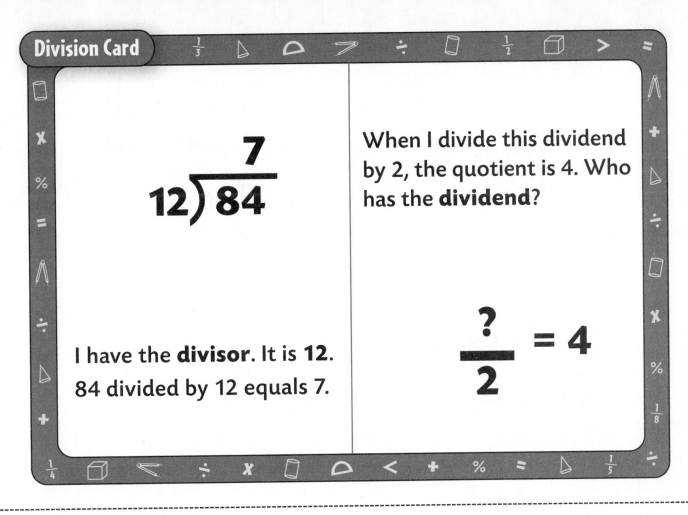

Division Card

$$\begin{array}{r} 7 \\ 12{\overline{\smash{)}84}} \end{array}$$

I have the **divisor**. It is **12**.
84 divided by 12 equals 7.

When I divide this dividend by 2, the quotient is 4. Who has the **dividend**?

$$\frac{?}{2} = 4$$

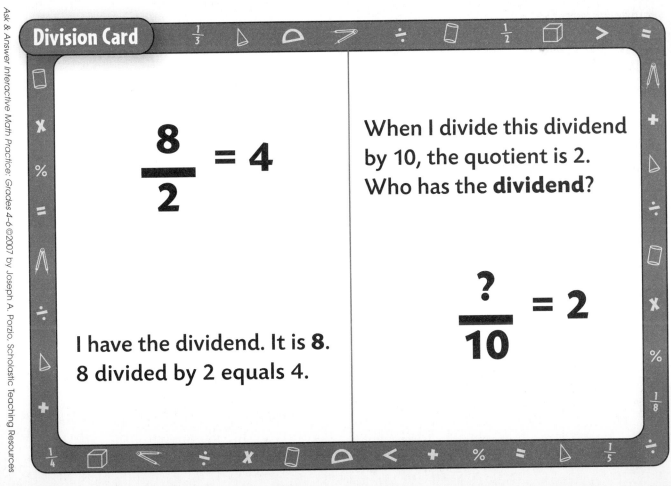

Division Card

$$\frac{8}{2} = 4$$

I have the dividend. It is **8**.
8 divided by 2 equals 4.

When I divide this dividend by 10, the quotient is 2. Who has the **dividend**?

$$\frac{?}{10} = 2$$

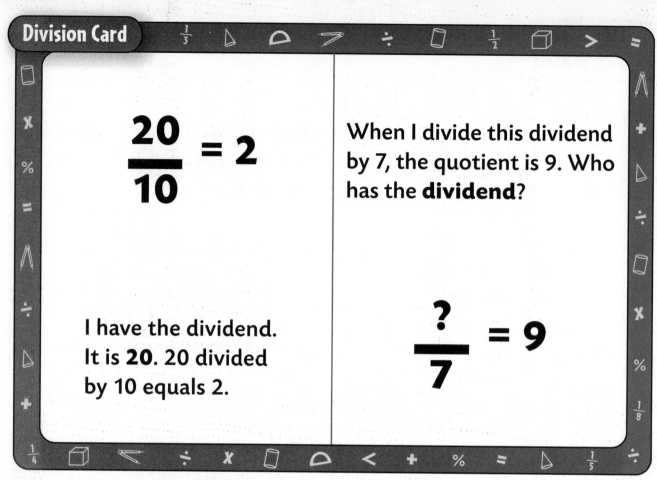

$$\frac{20}{10} = 2$$

When I divide this dividend by 7, the quotient is 9. Who has the **dividend**?

I have the dividend. It is **20**. 20 divided by 10 equals 2.

$$\frac{?}{7} = 9$$

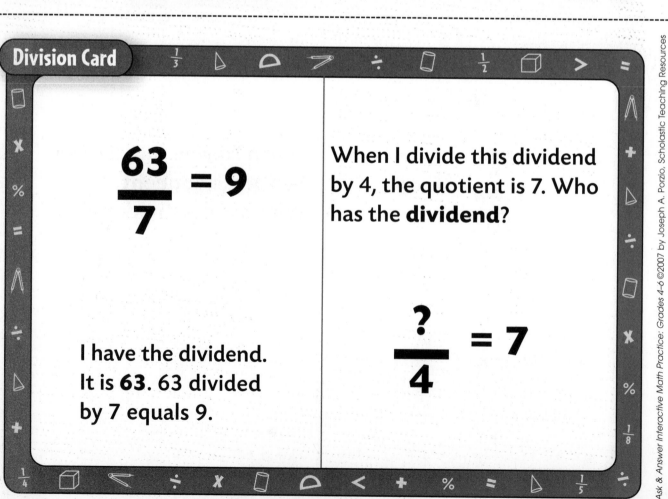

$$\frac{63}{7} = 9$$

When I divide this dividend by 4, the quotient is 7. Who has the **dividend**?

I have the dividend. It is **63**. 63 divided by 7 equals 9.

$$\frac{?}{4} = 7$$

Ask & Answer Interactive Math Practice: Grades 4–6 ©2007 by Joseph A. Porzio, Scholastic Teaching Resources

Ask & Answer Interactive Math Practice: Grades 4–6 ©2007 by Joseph A. Porzio, Scholastic Teaching Resources

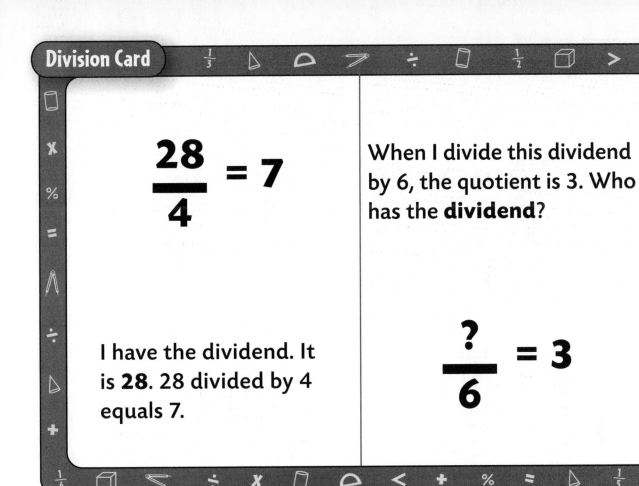

Division Card

$$\frac{28}{4} = 7$$

When I divide this dividend by 6, the quotient is 3. Who has the **dividend**?

I have the dividend. It is **28**. 28 divided by 4 equals 7.

$$\frac{?}{6} = 3$$

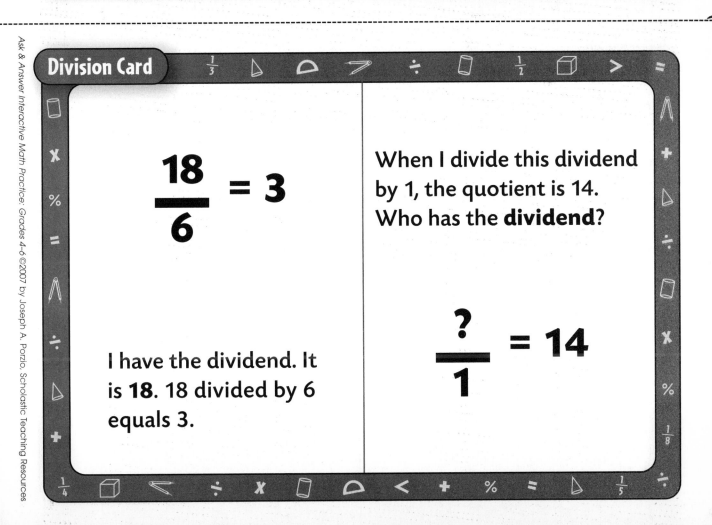

Division Card

$$\frac{18}{6} = 3$$

When I divide this dividend by 1, the quotient is 14. Who has the **dividend**?

I have the dividend. It is **18**. 18 divided by 6 equals 3.

$$\frac{?}{1} = 14$$

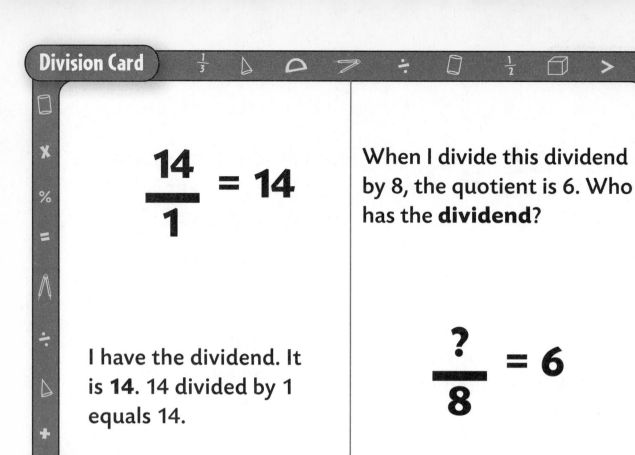

$$\frac{14}{1} = 14$$

When I divide this dividend by 8, the quotient is 6. Who has the **dividend**?

I have the dividend. It is **14**. 14 divided by 1 equals 14.

$$\frac{?}{8} = 6$$

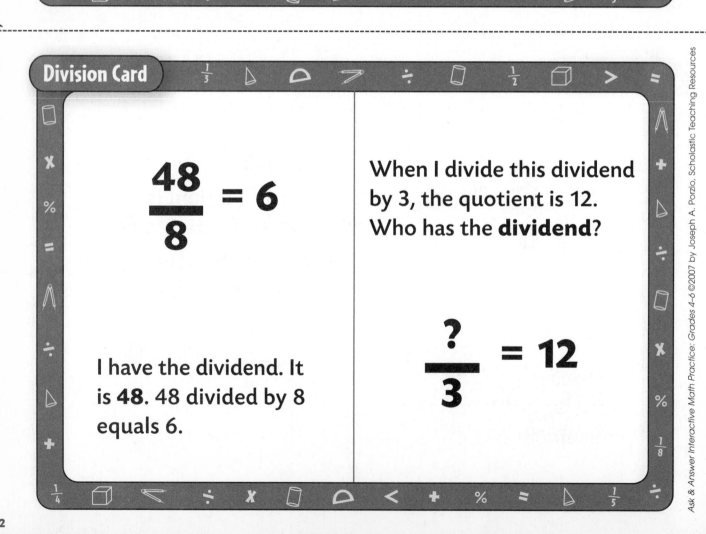

$$\frac{48}{8} = 6$$

When I divide this dividend by 3, the quotient is 12. Who has the **dividend**?

I have the dividend. It is **48**. 48 divided by 8 equals 6.

$$\frac{?}{3} = 12$$

Ask & Answer Interactive Math Practice: Grades 4–6 ©2007 by Joseph A. Porzio, Scholastic Teaching Resources

Ask & Answer Interactive Math Practice: Grades 4-6 ©2007 by Joseph A. Porzio, Scholastic Teaching Resources

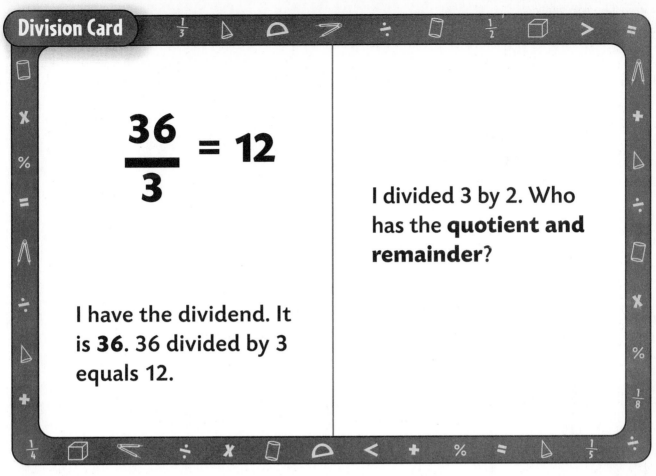

Division Card

$$\frac{36}{3} = 12$$

I divided 3 by 2. Who has the **quotient and remainder**?

I have the dividend. It is **36**. 36 divided by 3 equals 12.

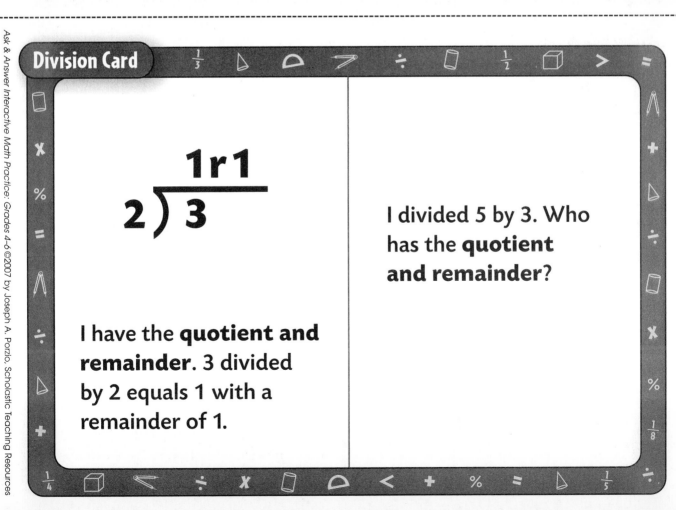

Division Card

$$2\overline{)3}^{\,1r1}$$

I divided 5 by 3. Who has the **quotient and remainder**?

I have the **quotient and remainder**. 3 divided by 2 equals 1 with a remainder of 1.

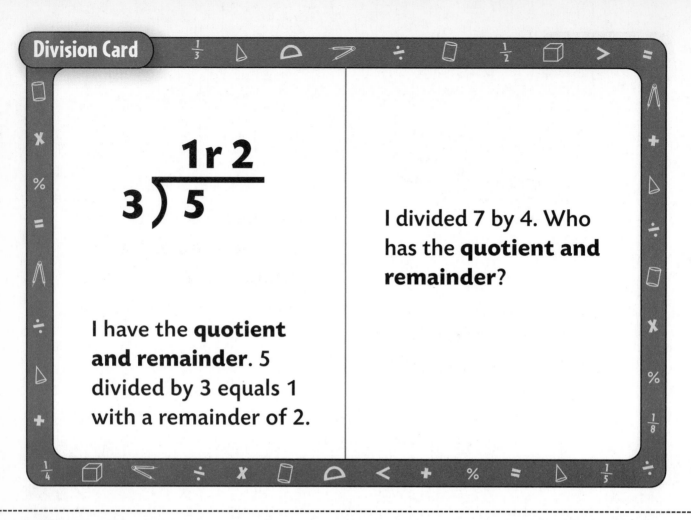

Division Card

$$3\overline{\smash{)}5}^{\,1r\,2}$$

I have the **quotient and remainder**. 5 divided by 3 equals 1 with a remainder of 2.

I divided 7 by 4. Who has the **quotient and remainder**?

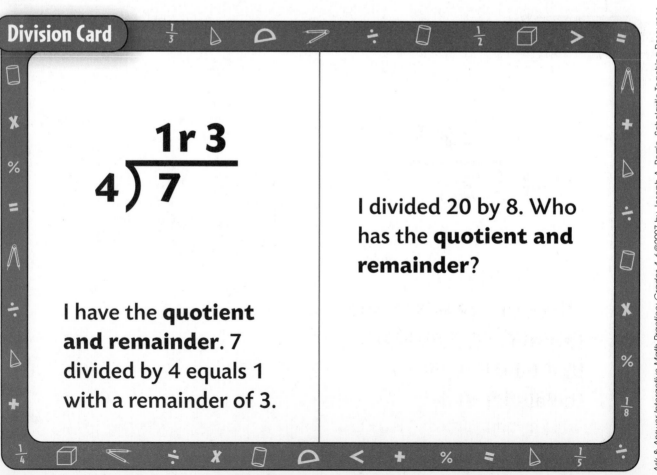

Division Card

$$4\overline{\smash{)}7}^{\,1r\,3}$$

I have the **quotient and remainder**. 7 divided by 4 equals 1 with a remainder of 3.

I divided 20 by 8. Who has the **quotient and remainder**?

Ask & Answer Interactive Math Practice: Grades 4–6 ©2007 by Joseph A. Porzio, Scholastic Teaching Resources

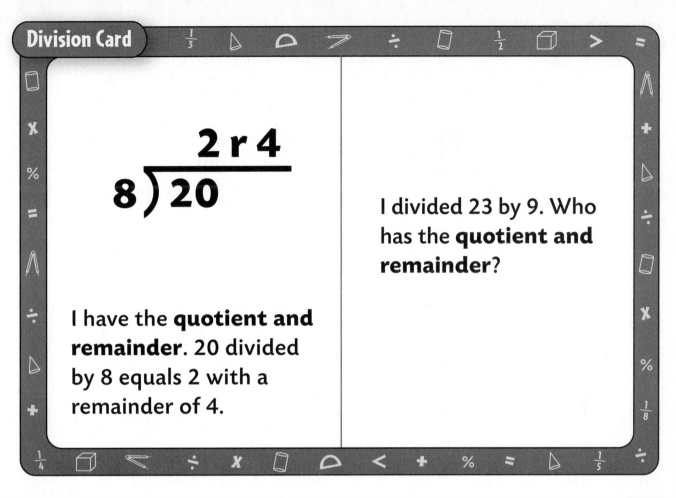

Division Card

$$8 \overline{)20} ^{2\,r\,4}$$

I divided 23 by 9. Who has the **quotient and remainder**?

I have the **quotient and remainder**. 20 divided by 8 equals 2 with a remainder of 4.

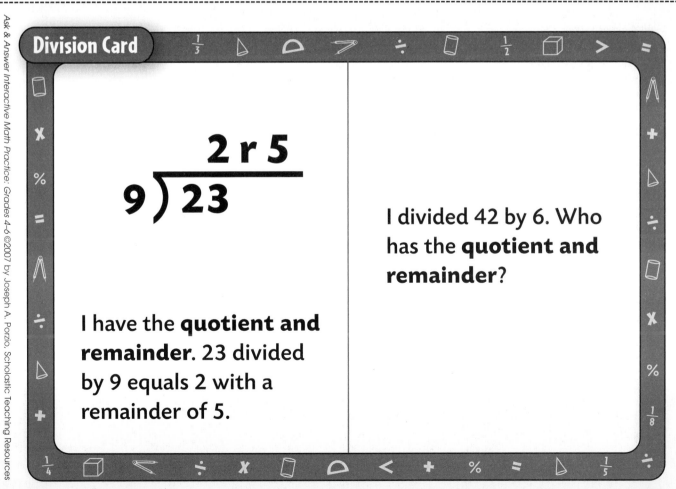

Division Card

$$9 \overline{)23} ^{2\,r\,5}$$

I divided 42 by 6. Who has the **quotient and remainder**?

I have the **quotient and remainder**. 23 divided by 9 equals 2 with a remainder of 5.

$$\begin{array}{r} 7\,r\,0 \\ 6\overline{)42} \end{array}$$

I have the **quotient and remainder**. 42 divided by 6 equals 7 with no remainder.

Kendall opened a bag of W&W candies and counted 54 candies in all. The candies came in 6 colors. Each color had the same number of candies. Who has **the number of candies in each color**?

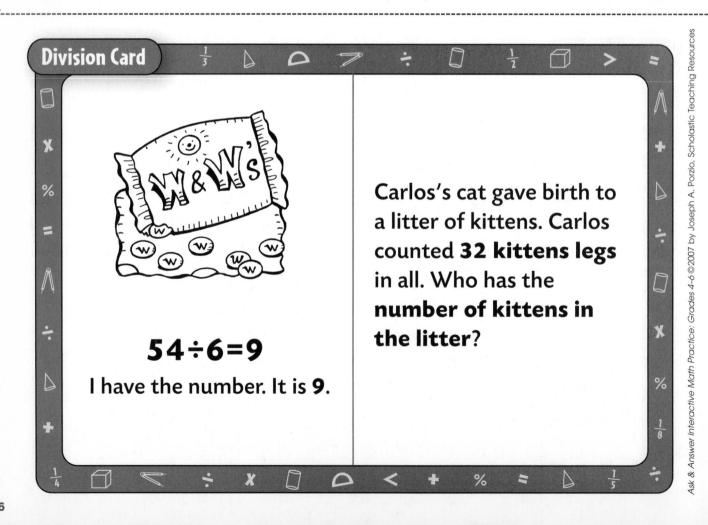

$$54 \div 6 = 9$$

I have the number. It is **9**.

Carlos's cat gave birth to a litter of kittens. Carlos counted **32 kittens legs** in all. Who has the **number of kittens in the litter**?

Ask & Answer Interactive Math Practice: Grades 4–6 © 2007 by Joseph A. Porzio, Scholastic Teaching Resources

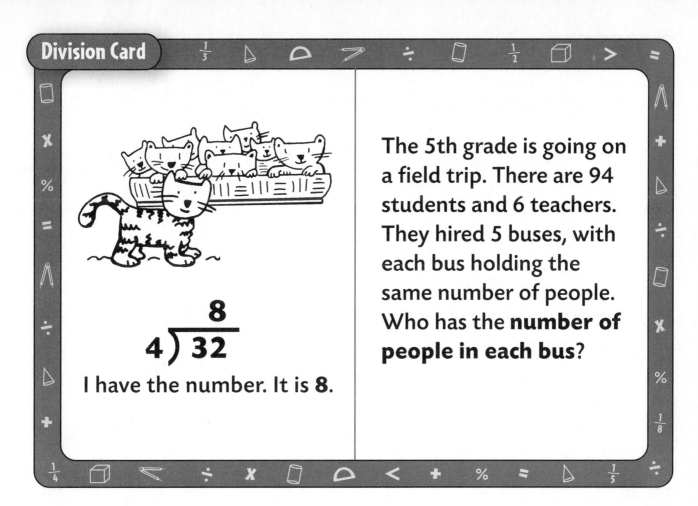

$$4\overline{)32} \quad \overset{8}{}$$

I have the number. It is **8**.

The 5th grade is going on a field trip. There are 94 students and 6 teachers. They hired 5 buses, with each bus holding the same number of people. Who has the **number of people in each bus**?

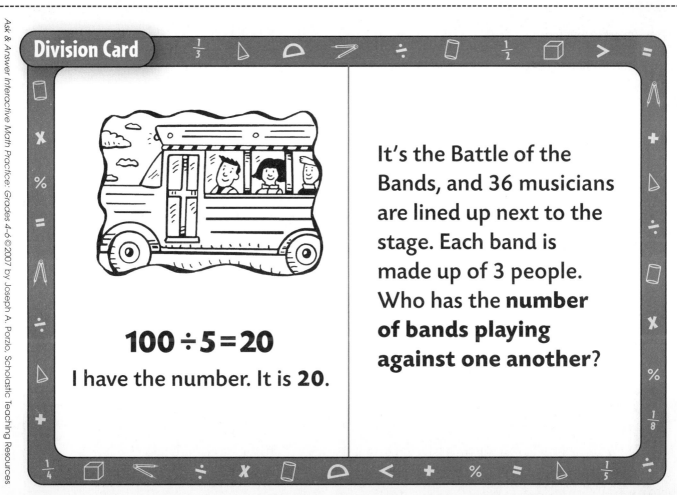

$$100 \div 5 = 20$$

I have the number. It is **20**.

It's the Battle of the Bands, and 36 musicians are lined up next to the stage. Each band is made up of 3 people. Who has the **number of bands playing against one another**?

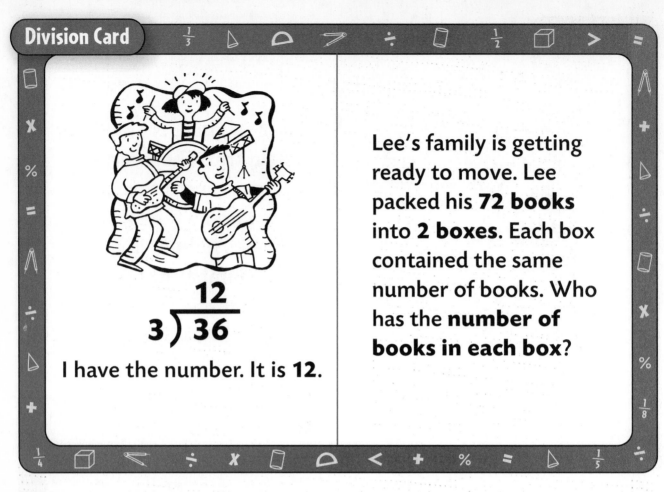

$$\begin{array}{r} 12 \\ 3\overline{)\,36} \end{array}$$

I have the number. It is **12**.

Lee's family is getting ready to move. Lee packed his **72 books** into **2 boxes**. Each box contained the same number of books. Who has the **number of books in each box**?

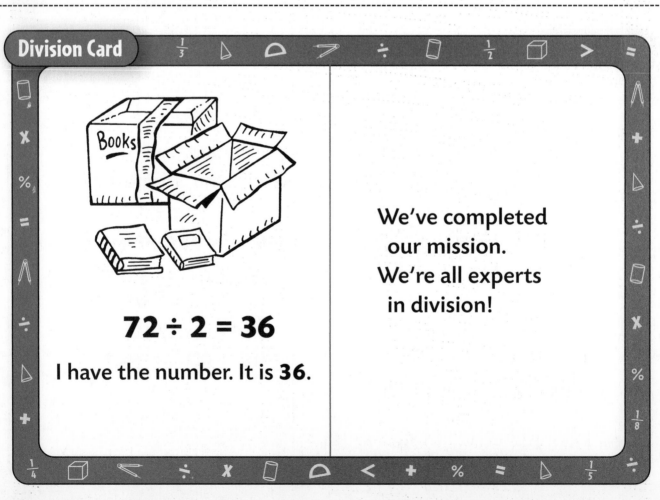

$$72 \div 2 = 36$$

I have the number. It is **36**.

We've completed our mission. We're all experts in division!

Ask & Answer Interactive Math Practice: Grades 4–6 © 2007 by Joseph A. Porzio, Scholastic Teaching Resources

Get ready for some action. It's time to review our **fractions**!

Who has the **rectangle** that is **one-half** ($\frac{1}{2}$) shaded?

Ask & Answer Interactive Math Practice: Grades 4–6 ©2007 by Joseph A. Porzio, Scholastic Teaching Resources

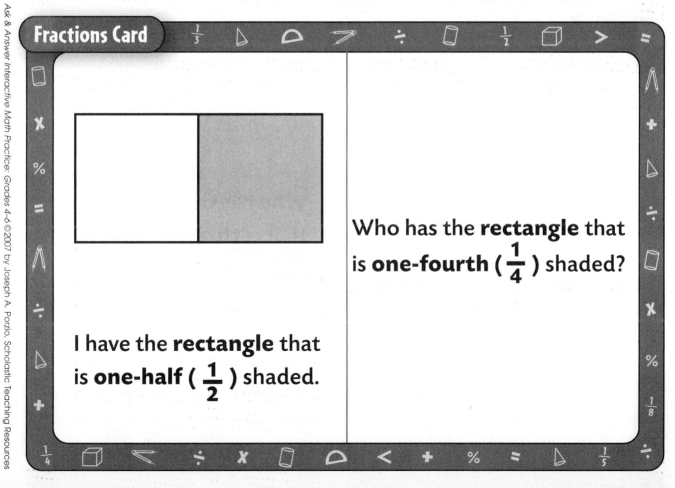

I have the **rectangle** that is **one-half** ($\frac{1}{2}$) shaded.

Who has the **rectangle** that is **one-fourth** ($\frac{1}{4}$) shaded?

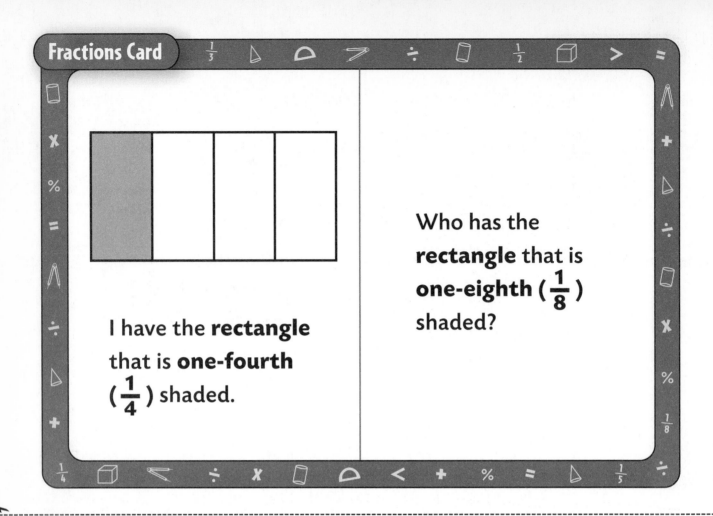

I have the **rectangle** that is **one-fourth** ($\frac{1}{4}$) shaded.

Who has the **rectangle** that is **one-eighth** ($\frac{1}{8}$) shaded?

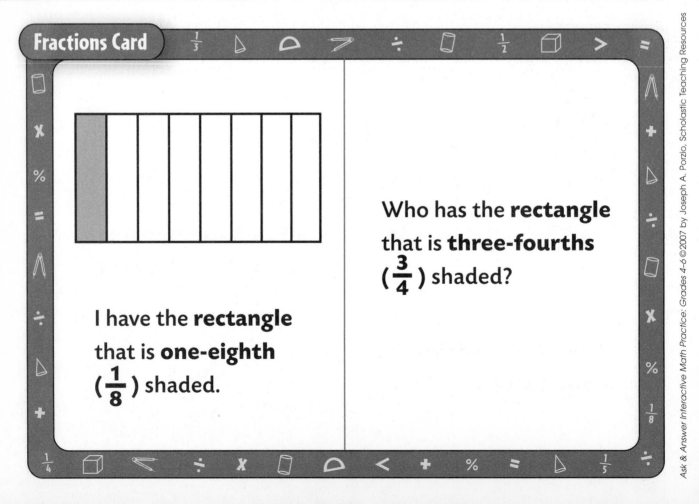

I have the **rectangle** that is **one-eighth** ($\frac{1}{8}$) shaded.

Who has the **rectangle** that is **three-fourths** ($\frac{3}{4}$) shaded?

Ask & Answer Interactive Math Practice: Grades 4–6 ©2007 by Joseph A. Porzio. Scholastic Teaching Resources

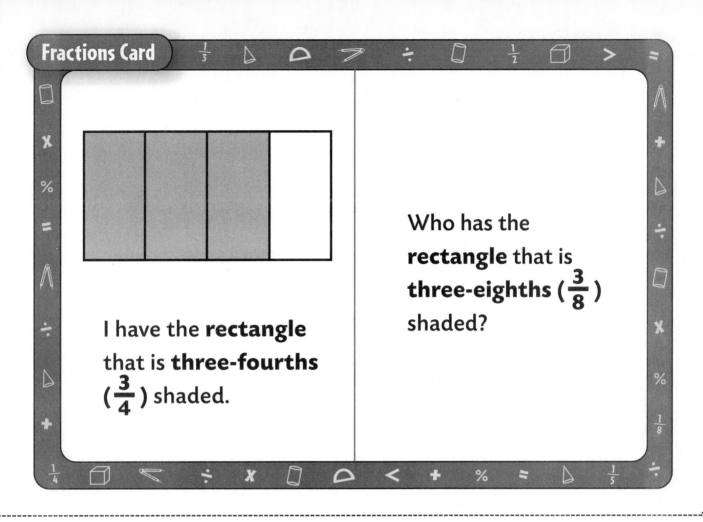

I have the **rectangle** that is **three-fourths** ($\frac{3}{4}$) shaded.

Who has the **rectangle** that is **three-eighths** ($\frac{3}{8}$) shaded?

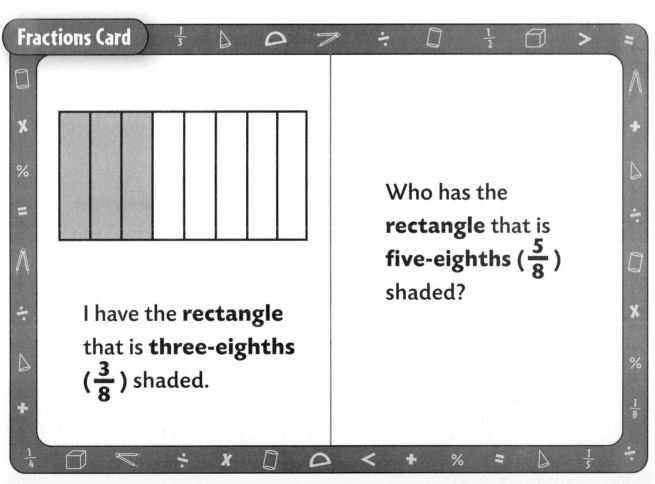

I have the **rectangle** that is **three-eighths** ($\frac{3}{8}$) shaded.

Who has the **rectangle** that is **five-eighths** ($\frac{5}{8}$) shaded?

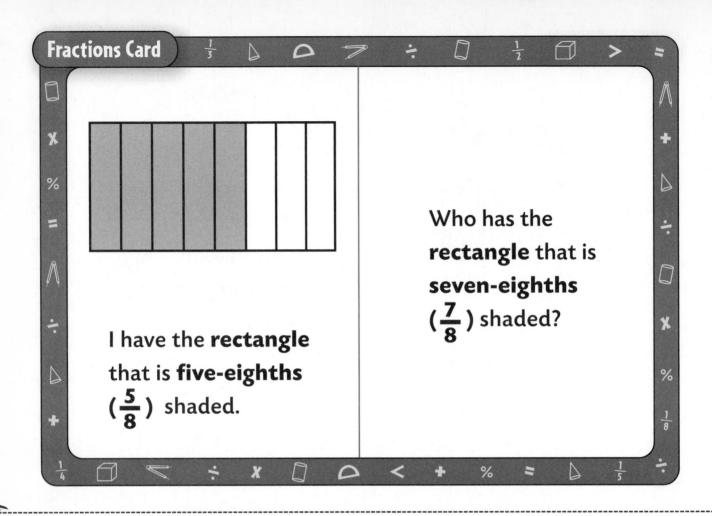

I have the **rectangle** that is **five-eighths** ($\frac{5}{8}$) shaded.

Who has the **rectangle** that is **seven-eighths** ($\frac{7}{8}$) shaded?

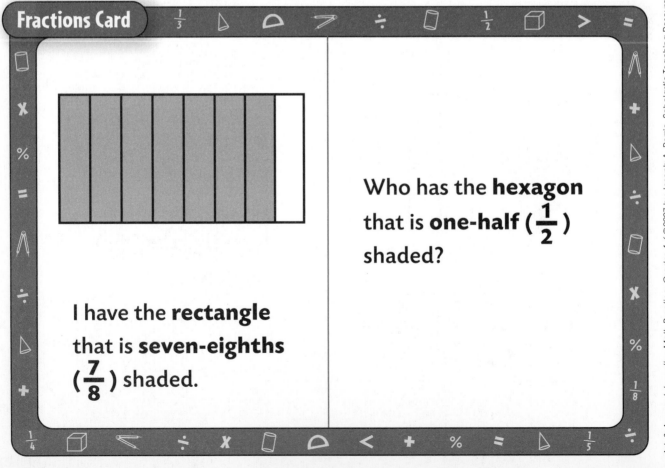

I have the **rectangle** that is **seven-eighths** ($\frac{7}{8}$) shaded.

Who has the **hexagon** that is **one-half** ($\frac{1}{2}$) shaded?

Ask & Answer Interactive Math Practice: Grades 4–6 ©2007 by Joseph A. Porzio, Scholastic Teaching Resources

Ask & Answer Interactive Math Practice: Grades 4–6 ©2007 by Joseph A. Porzio, Scholastic Teaching Resources

Fractions Card

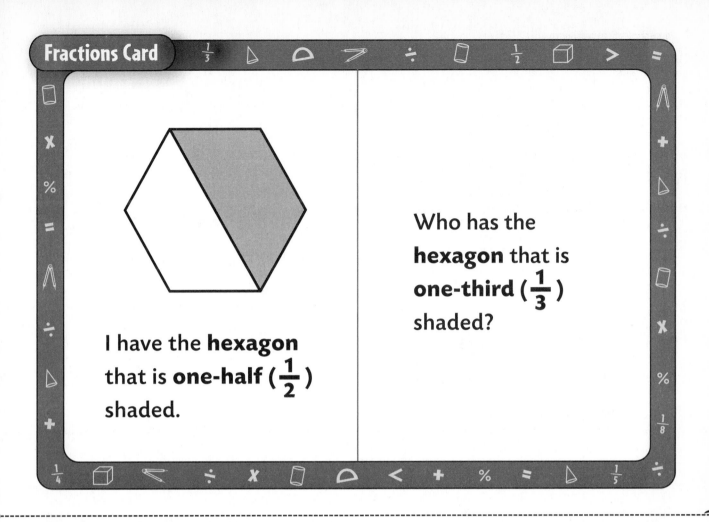

I have the **hexagon** that is **one-half ($\frac{1}{2}$)** shaded.

Who has the **hexagon** that is **one-third ($\frac{1}{3}$)** shaded?

Fractions Card

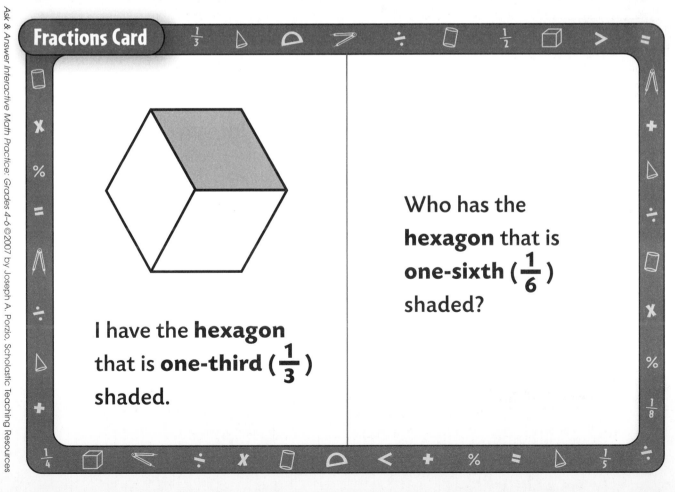

I have the **hexagon** that is **one-third ($\frac{1}{3}$)** shaded.

Who has the **hexagon** that is **one-sixth ($\frac{1}{6}$)** shaded?

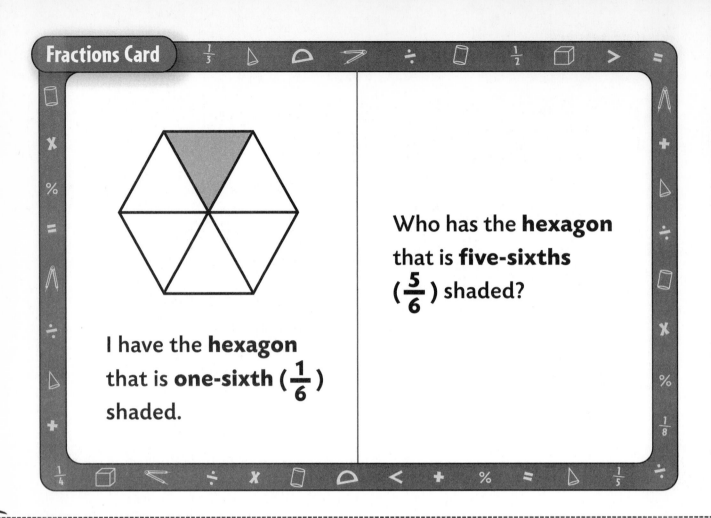

I have the **hexagon** that is **one-sixth ($\frac{1}{6}$)** shaded.

Who has the **hexagon** that is **five-sixths** ($\frac{5}{6}$) shaded?

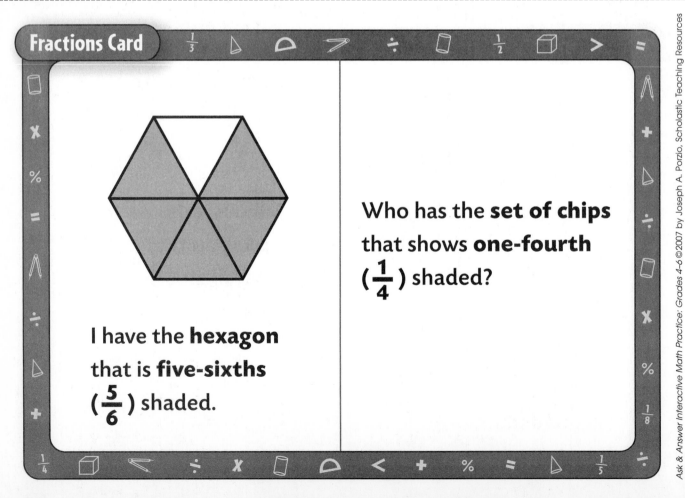

I have the **hexagon** that is **five-sixths** ($\frac{5}{6}$) shaded.

Who has the **set of chips** that shows **one-fourth** ($\frac{1}{4}$) shaded?

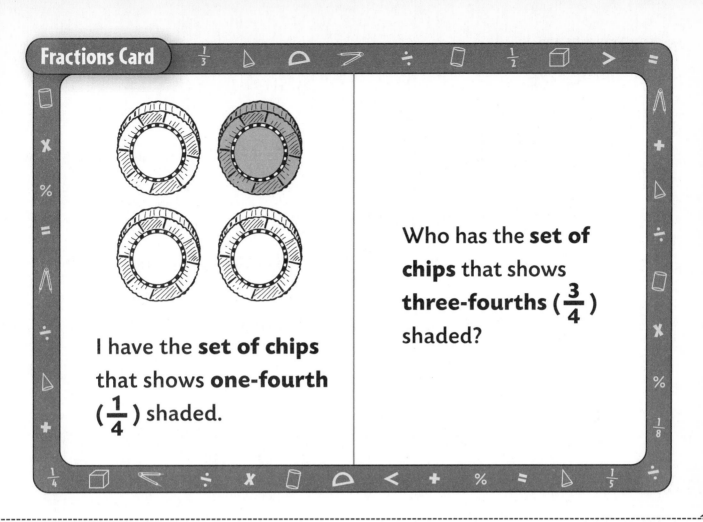

I have the **set of chips** that shows **one-fourth** ($\frac{1}{4}$) shaded.

Who has the **set of chips** that shows **three-fourths** ($\frac{3}{4}$) shaded?

Ask & Answer Interactive Math Practice: Grades 4–6 ©2007 by Joseph A. Porzio, Scholastic Teaching Resources

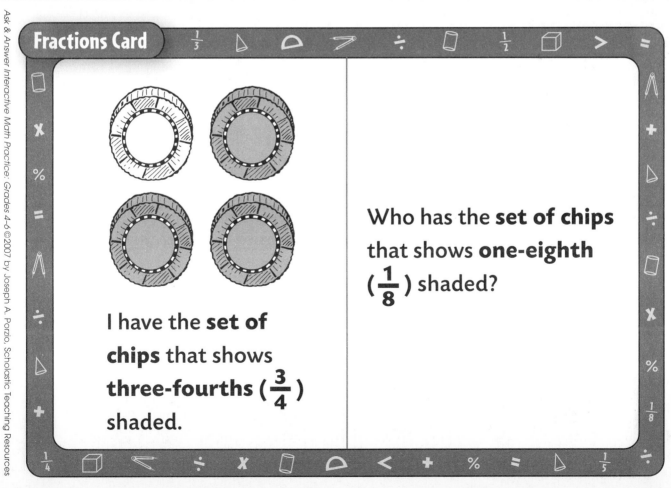

I have the **set of chips** that shows **three-fourths** ($\frac{3}{4}$) shaded.

Who has the **set of chips** that shows **one-eighth** ($\frac{1}{8}$) shaded?

Fractions Card

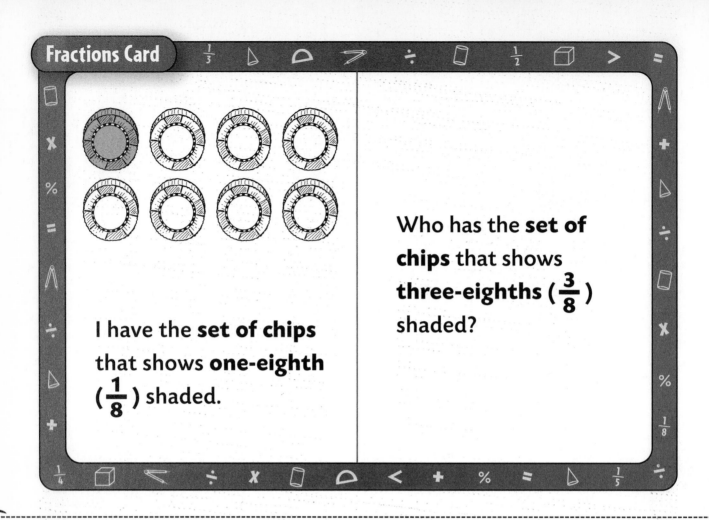

I have the **set of chips** that shows **one-eighth** ($\frac{1}{8}$) shaded.

Who has the **set of chips** that shows **three-eighths** ($\frac{3}{8}$) shaded?

Fractions Card

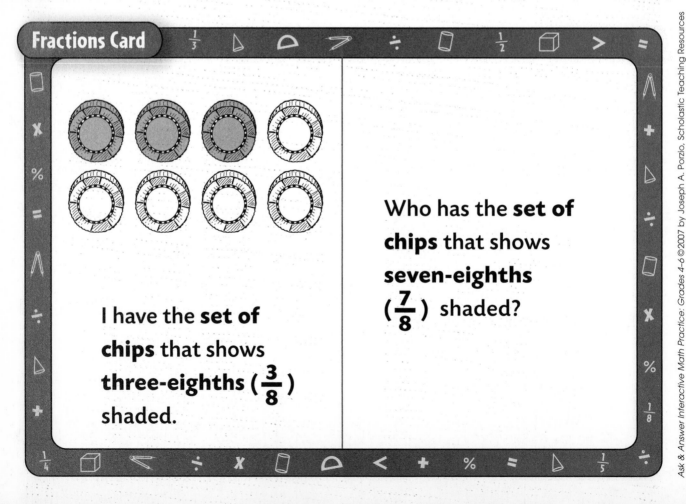

I have the **set of chips** that shows **three-eighths** ($\frac{3}{8}$) shaded.

Who has the **set of chips** that shows **seven-eighths** ($\frac{7}{8}$) shaded?

Ask & Answer Interactive Math Practice: Grades 4–6 ©2007 by Joseph A. Porzio, Scholastic Teaching Resources

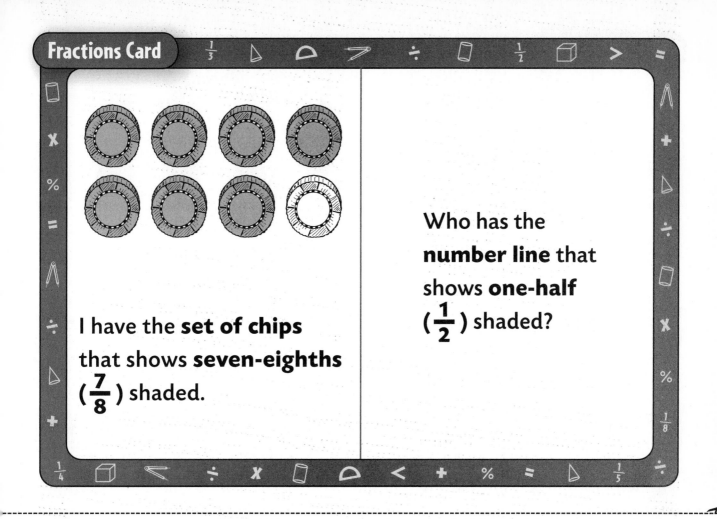

I have the **set of chips** that shows **seven-eighths** ($\frac{7}{8}$) shaded.

Who has the **number line** that shows **one-half** ($\frac{1}{2}$) shaded?

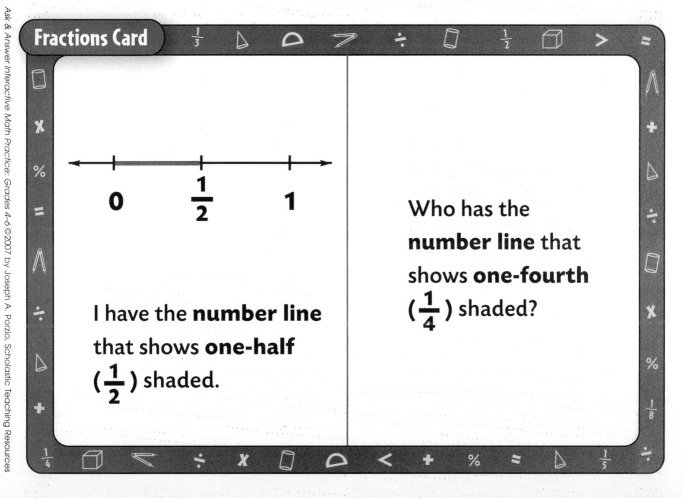

I have the **number line** that shows **one-half** ($\frac{1}{2}$) shaded.

Who has the **number line** that shows **one-fourth** ($\frac{1}{4}$) shaded?

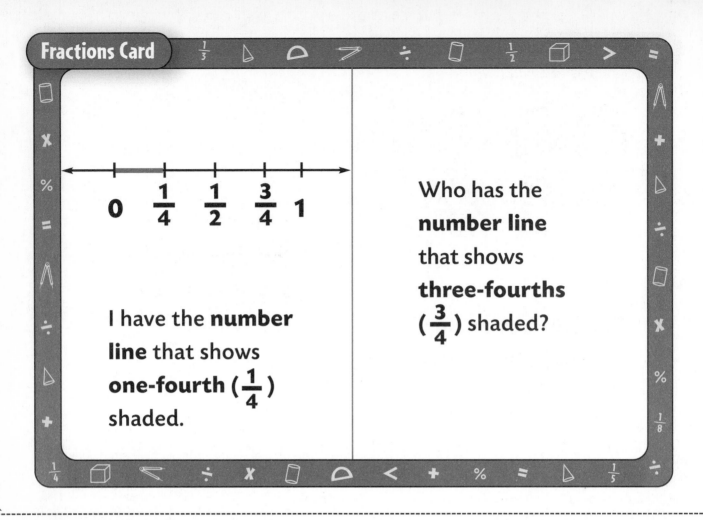

I have the **number line** that shows **one-fourth ($\frac{1}{4}$)** shaded.

Who has the **number line** that shows **three-fourths ($\frac{3}{4}$)** shaded?

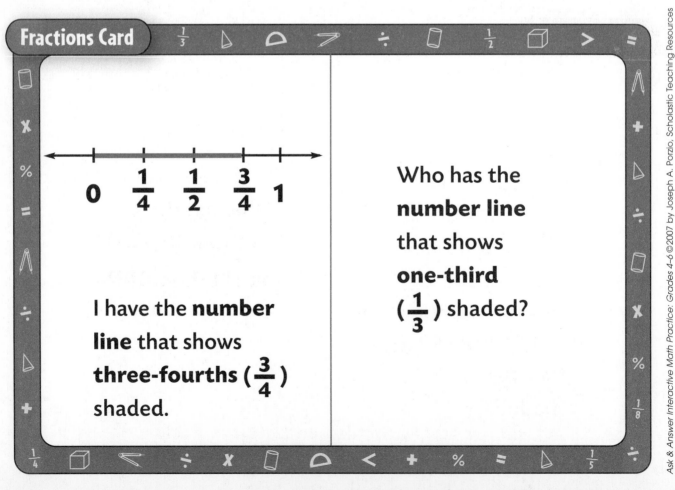

I have the **number line** that shows **three-fourths ($\frac{3}{4}$)** shaded.

Who has the **number line** that shows **one-third ($\frac{1}{3}$)** shaded?

Ask & Answer Interactive Math Practice: Grades 4–6 © 2007 by Joseph A. Porzio, Scholastic Teaching Resources

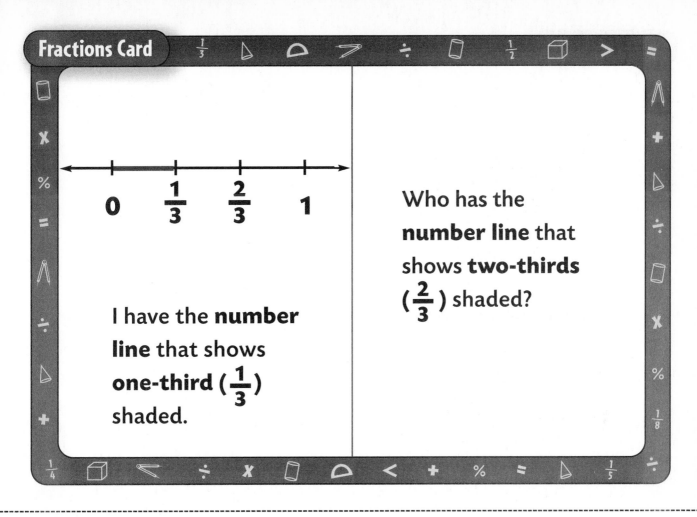

I have the **number line** that shows **one-third ($\frac{1}{3}$)** shaded.

Who has the **number line** that shows **two-thirds ($\frac{2}{3}$)** shaded?

Ask & Answer Interactive Math Practice: Grades 4–6 ©2007 by Joseph A. Porzio. Scholastic Teaching Resources

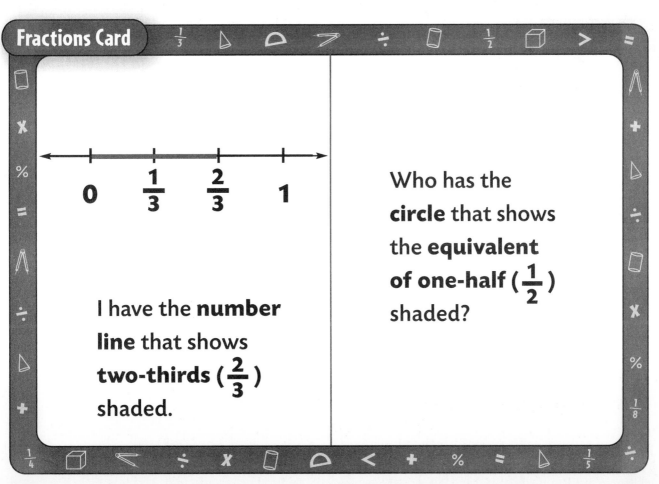

I have the **number line** that shows **two-thirds ($\frac{2}{3}$)** shaded.

Who has the **circle** that shows the **equivalent of one-half ($\frac{1}{2}$)** shaded?

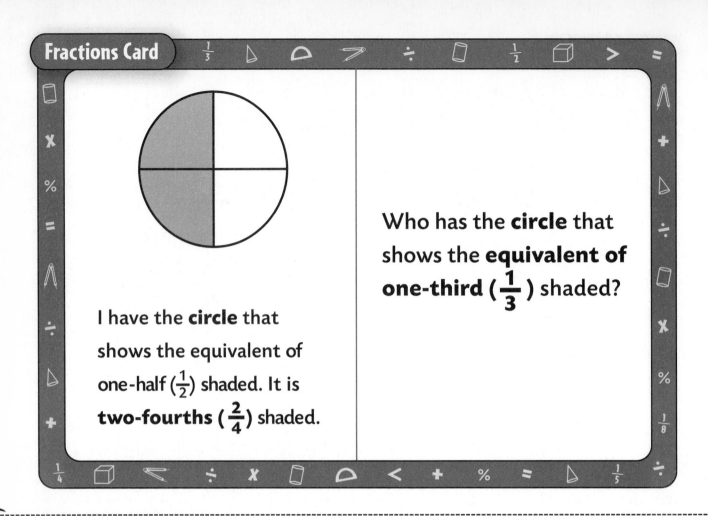

Fractions Card

I have the **circle** that shows the equivalent of one-half ($\frac{1}{2}$) shaded. It is **two-fourths ($\frac{2}{4}$)** shaded.

Who has the **circle** that shows the **equivalent of one-third ($\frac{1}{3}$)** shaded?

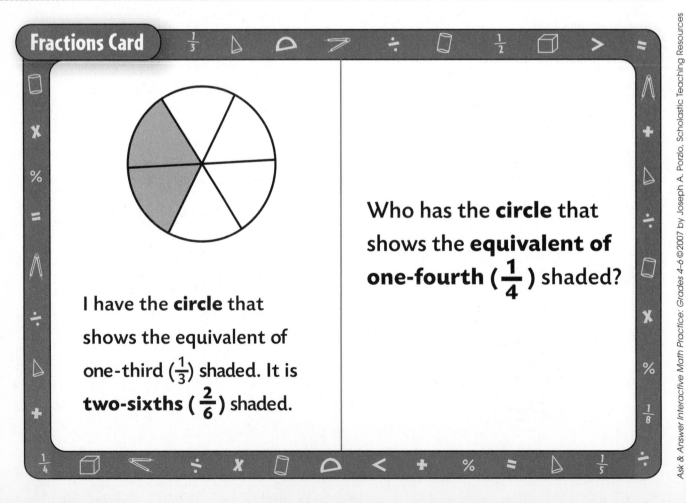

Fractions Card

I have the **circle** that shows the equivalent of one-third ($\frac{1}{3}$) shaded. It is **two-sixths ($\frac{2}{6}$)** shaded.

Who has the **circle** that shows the **equivalent of one-fourth ($\frac{1}{4}$)** shaded?

Ask & Answer Interactive Math Practice: Grades 4–6 ©2007 by Joseph A. Porzio. Scholastic Teaching Resources

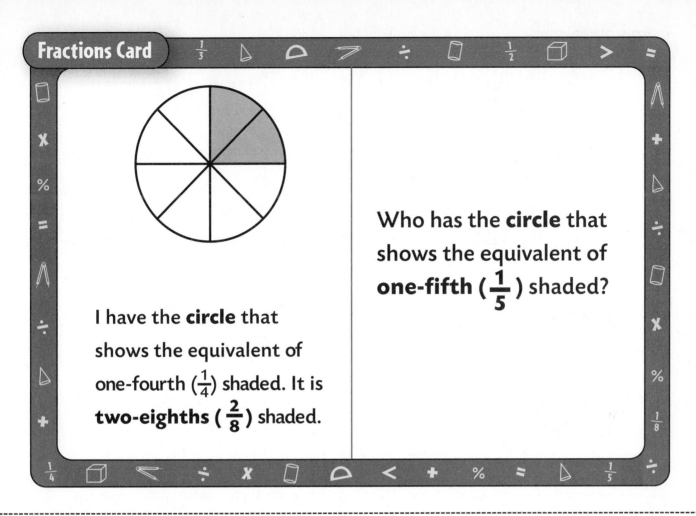

Fractions Card

I have the **circle** that shows the equivalent of one-fourth ($\frac{1}{4}$) shaded. It is **two-eighths** ($\frac{2}{8}$) shaded.

Who has the **circle** that shows the equivalent of **one-fifth** ($\frac{1}{5}$) shaded?

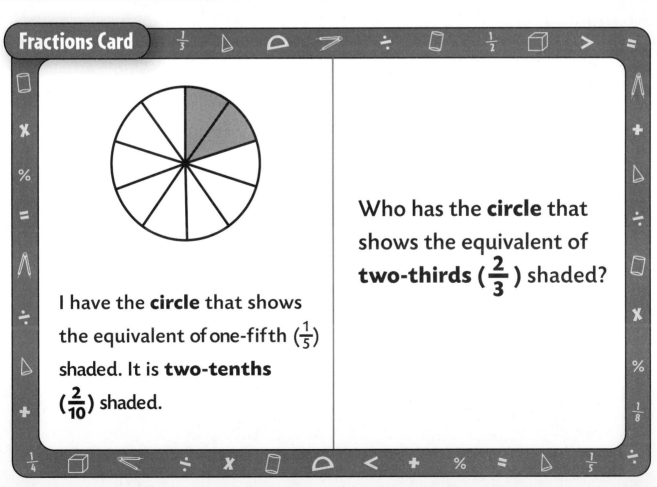

Fractions Card

I have the **circle** that shows the equivalent of one-fifth ($\frac{1}{5}$) shaded. It is **two-tenths** ($\frac{2}{10}$) shaded.

Who has the **circle** that shows the equivalent of **two-thirds** ($\frac{2}{3}$) shaded?

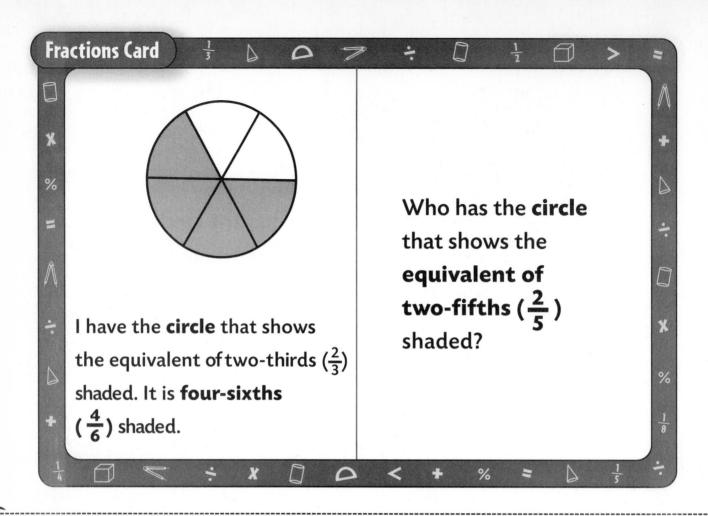

I have the **circle** that shows the equivalent of two-thirds ($\frac{2}{3}$) shaded. It is **four-sixths** ($\frac{4}{6}$) shaded.

Who has the **circle** that shows the **equivalent of two-fifths** ($\frac{2}{5}$) shaded?

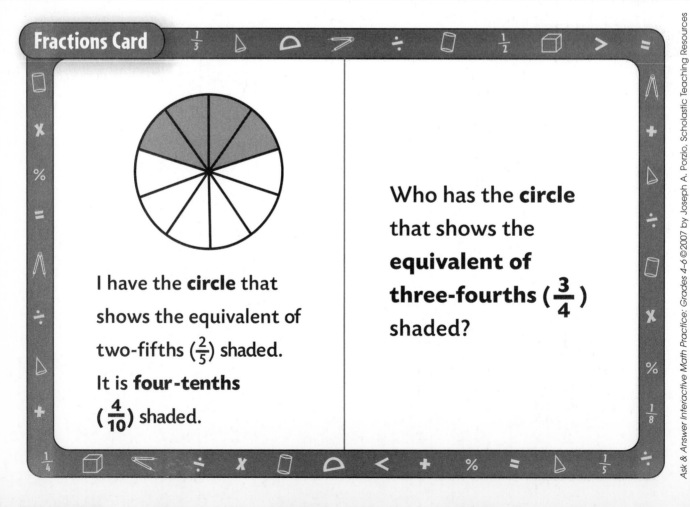

I have the **circle** that shows the equivalent of two-fifths ($\frac{2}{5}$) shaded. It is **four-tenths** ($\frac{4}{10}$) shaded.

Who has the **circle** that shows the **equivalent of three-fourths** ($\frac{3}{4}$) shaded?

Ask & Answer Interactive Math Practice: Grades 4–6 ©2007 by Joseph A. Porzio, Scholastic Teaching Resources

Fractions Card

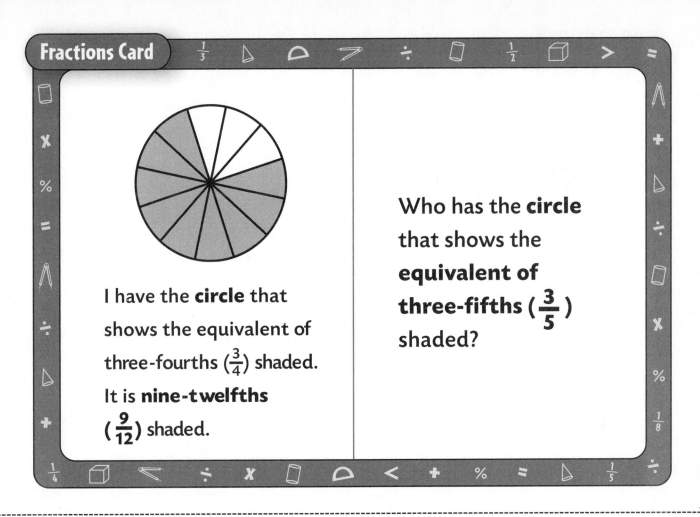

I have the **circle** that shows the equivalent of three-fourths ($\frac{3}{4}$) shaded. It is **nine-twelfths** ($\frac{9}{12}$) shaded.

Who has the **circle** that shows the **equivalent of three-fifths** ($\frac{3}{5}$) shaded?

Fractions Card

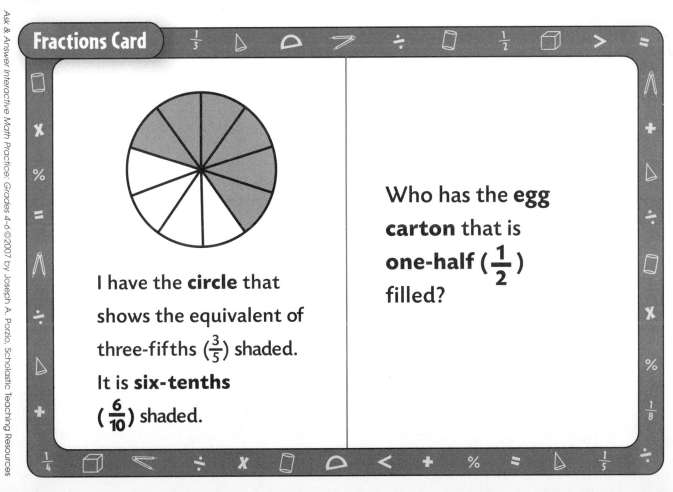

I have the **circle** that shows the equivalent of three-fifths ($\frac{3}{5}$) shaded. It is **six-tenths** ($\frac{6}{10}$) shaded.

Who has the **egg carton** that is **one-half** ($\frac{1}{2}$) filled?

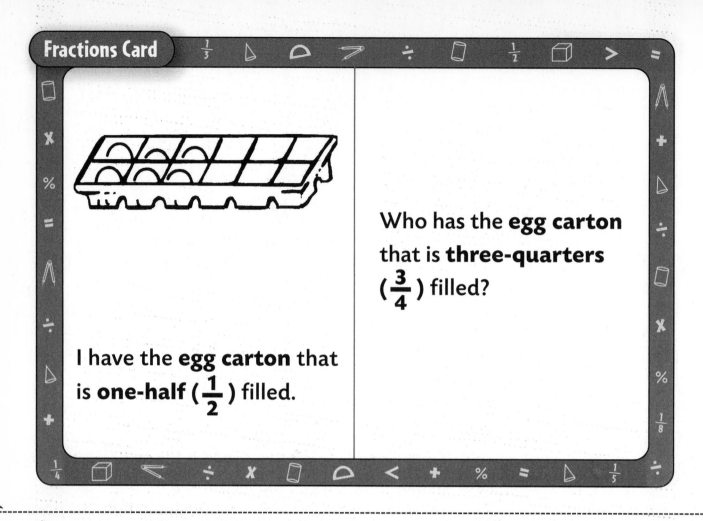

Who has the **egg carton** that is **three-quarters** ($\frac{3}{4}$) filled?

I have the **egg carton** that is **one-half** ($\frac{1}{2}$) filled.

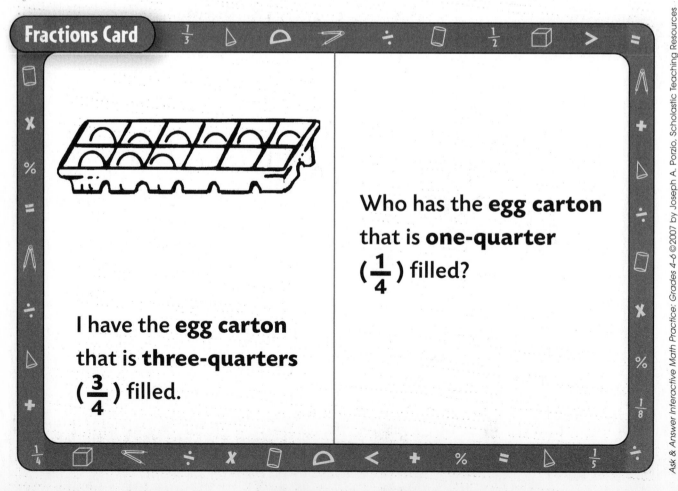

Who has the **egg carton** that is **one-quarter** ($\frac{1}{4}$) filled?

I have the **egg carton** that is **three-quarters** ($\frac{3}{4}$) filled.

Ask & Answer Interactive Math Practice: Grades 4–6 ©2007 by Joseph A. Porzio, Scholastic Teaching Resources

Fractions Card

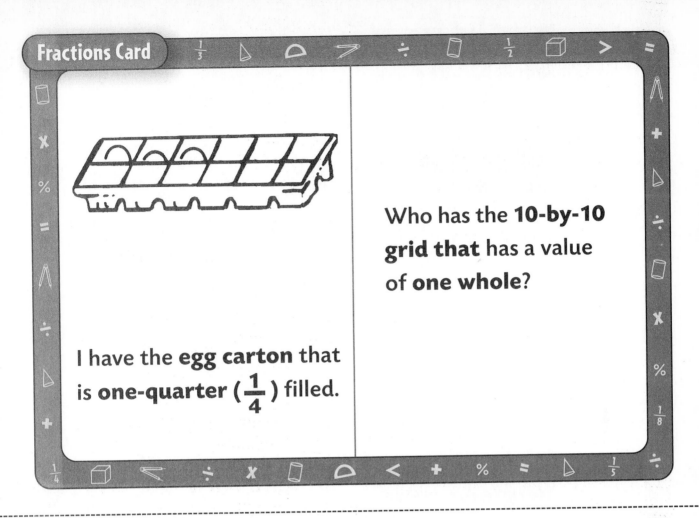

I have the **egg carton** that is **one-quarter** ($\frac{1}{4}$) filled.

Who has the **10-by-10 grid that** has a value of **one whole**?

Fractions Card

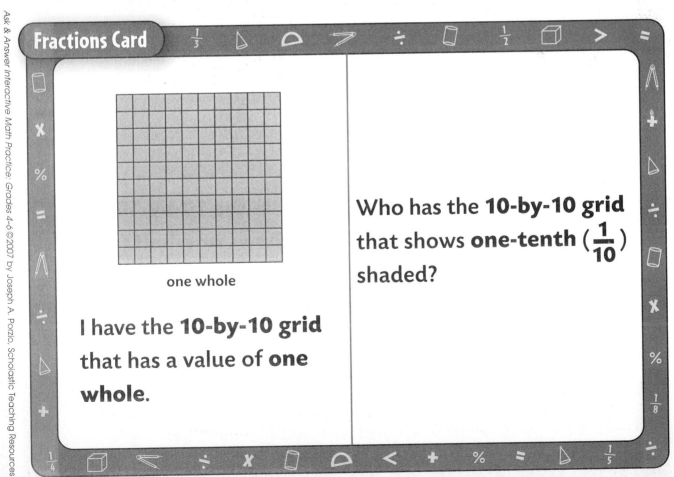

one whole

I have the **10-by-10 grid** that has a value of **one whole**.

Who has the **10-by-10 grid** that shows **one-tenth** ($\frac{1}{10}$) shaded?

Fractions Card

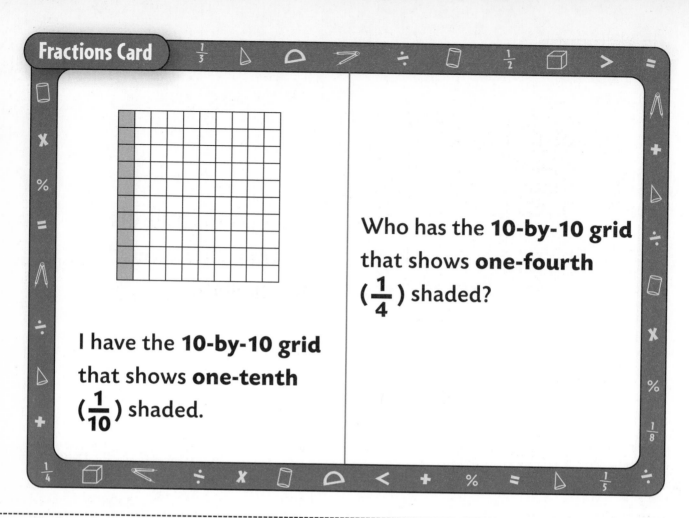

I have the **10-by-10 grid** that shows **one-tenth** ($\frac{1}{10}$) shaded.

Who has the **10-by-10 grid** that shows **one-fourth** ($\frac{1}{4}$) shaded?

Fractions Card

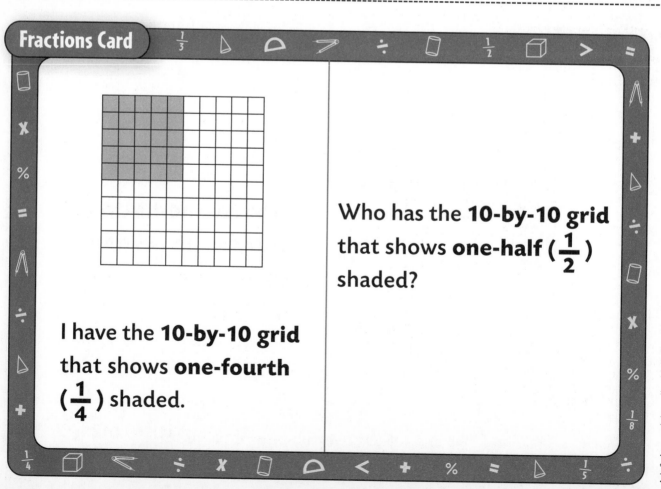

I have the **10-by-10 grid** that shows **one-fourth** ($\frac{1}{4}$) shaded.

Who has the **10-by-10 grid** that shows **one-half** ($\frac{1}{2}$) shaded?

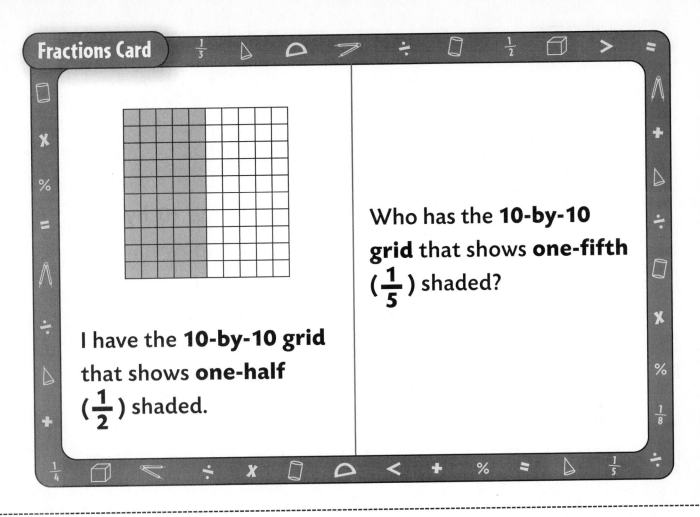

Fractions Card

I have the **10-by-10 grid** that shows **one-half** ($\frac{1}{2}$) shaded.

Who has the **10-by-10 grid** that shows **one-fifth** ($\frac{1}{5}$) shaded?

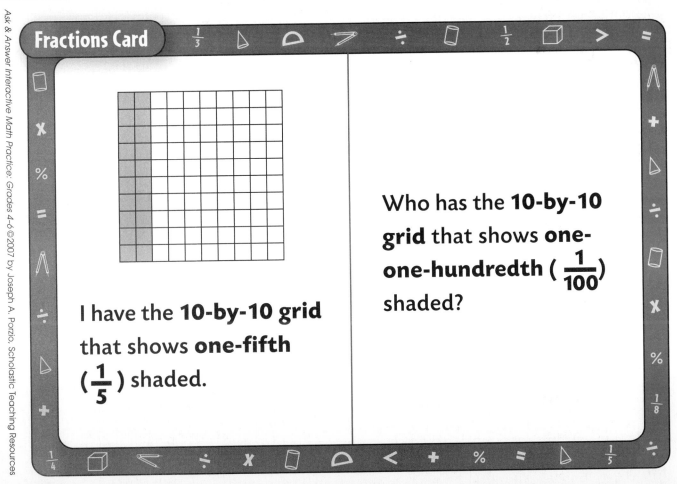

Fractions Card

I have the **10-by-10 grid** that shows **one-fifth** ($\frac{1}{5}$) shaded.

Who has the **10-by-10 grid** that shows **one-one-hundredth** ($\frac{1}{100}$) shaded?

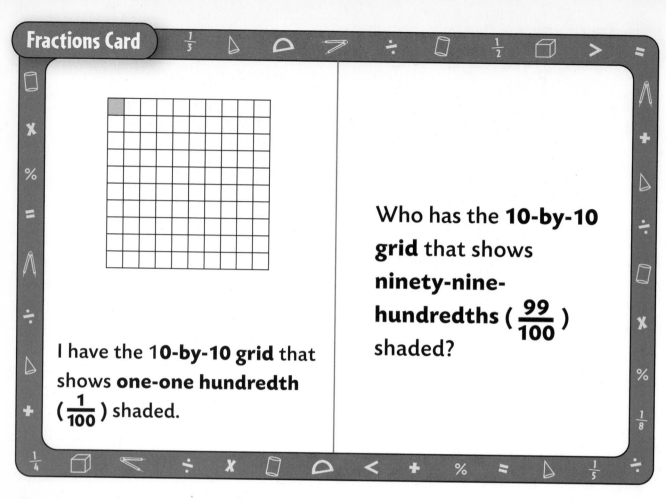

Fractions Card

I have the 10-by-10 grid that shows **one-one hundredth** ($\frac{1}{100}$) shaded.

Who has the **10-by-10 grid** that shows **ninety-nine-hundredths** ($\frac{99}{100}$) shaded?

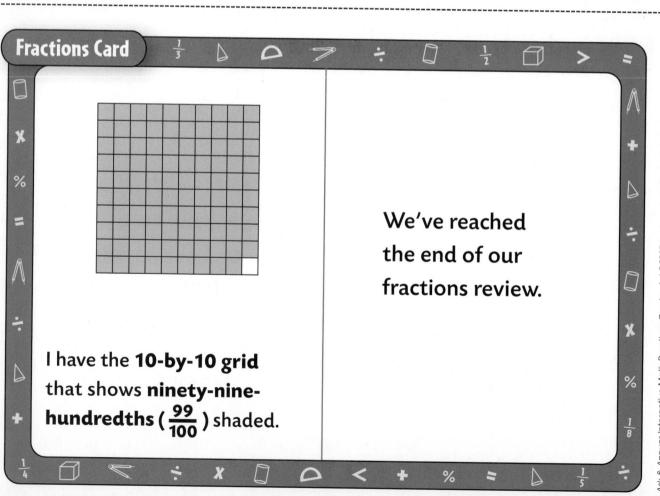

Fractions Card

I have the **10-by-10 grid** that shows **ninety-nine-hundredths** ($\frac{99}{100}$) shaded.

We've reached the end of our fractions review.

Ask & Answer Interactive Math Practice: Grades 4–6 © 2007 by Joseph A. Porzio, Scholastic Teaching Resources

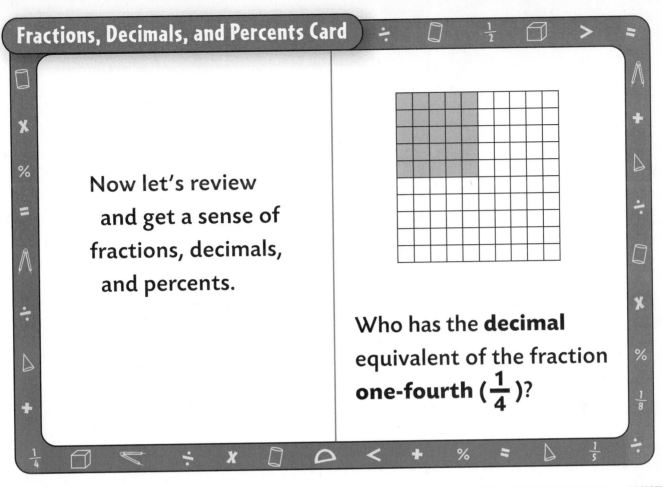

Now let's review and get a sense of fractions, decimals, and percents.

Who has the **decimal** equivalent of the fraction **one-fourth** ($\frac{1}{4}$)?

Ask & Answer Interactive Math Practice: Grades 4–6 ©2007 by Joseph A. Porzio, Scholastic Teaching Resources

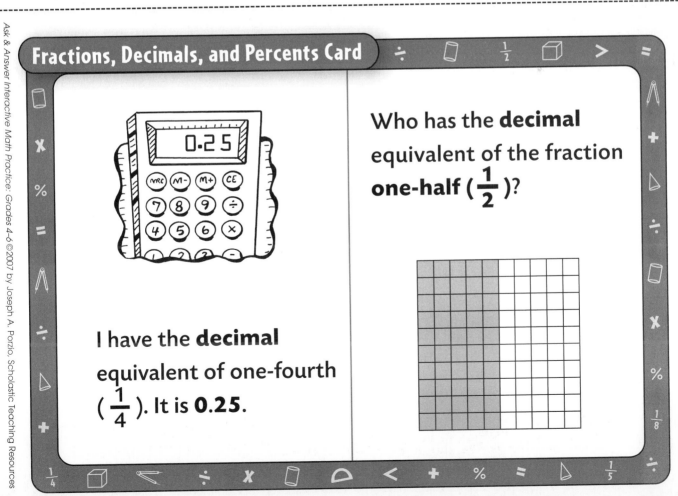

Who has the **decimal** equivalent of the fraction **one-half** ($\frac{1}{2}$)?

I have the **decimal** equivalent of one-fourth ($\frac{1}{4}$). It is **0.25**.

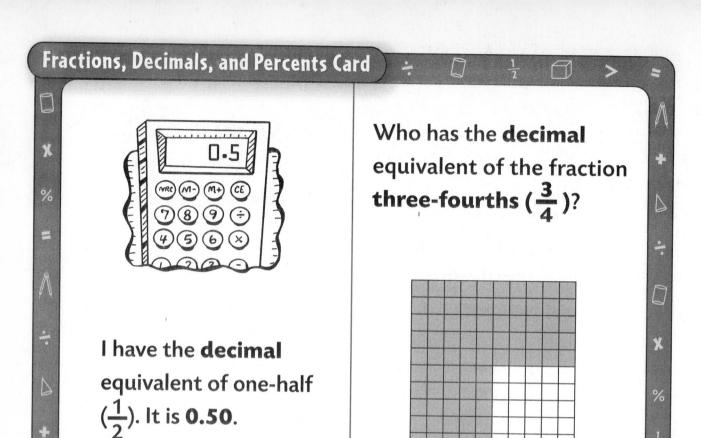

Who has the **decimal** equivalent of the fraction **three-fourths** ($\frac{3}{4}$)?

I have the **decimal** equivalent of one-half ($\frac{1}{2}$). It is **0.50**.

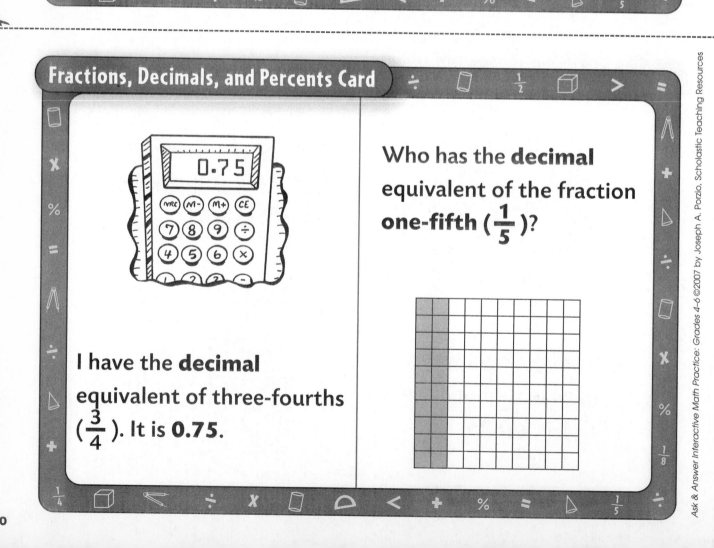

Who has the **decimal** equivalent of the fraction **one-fifth** ($\frac{1}{5}$)?

I have the **decimal** equivalent of three-fourths ($\frac{3}{4}$). It is **0.75**.

Ask & Answer Interactive Math Practice: Grades 4–6 ©2007 by Joseph A. Porzio, Scholastic Teaching Resources

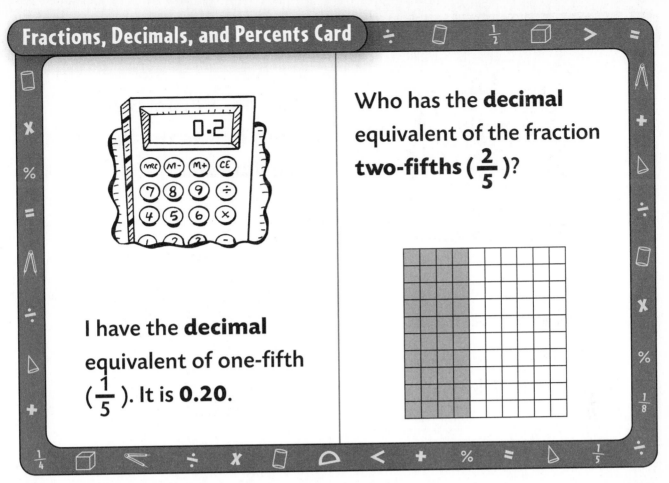

Who has the **decimal** equivalent of the fraction **two-fifths** ($\frac{2}{5}$)?

I have the **decimal** equivalent of one-fifth ($\frac{1}{5}$). It is **0.20**.

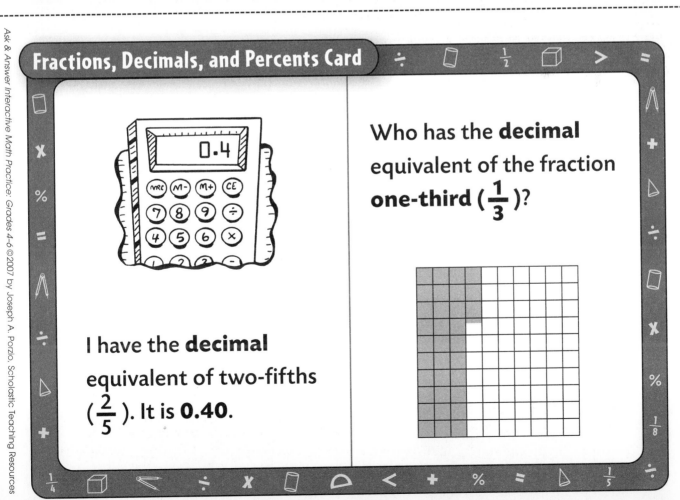

Who has the **decimal** equivalent of the fraction **one-third** ($\frac{1}{3}$)?

I have the **decimal** equivalent of two-fifths ($\frac{2}{5}$). It is **0.40**.

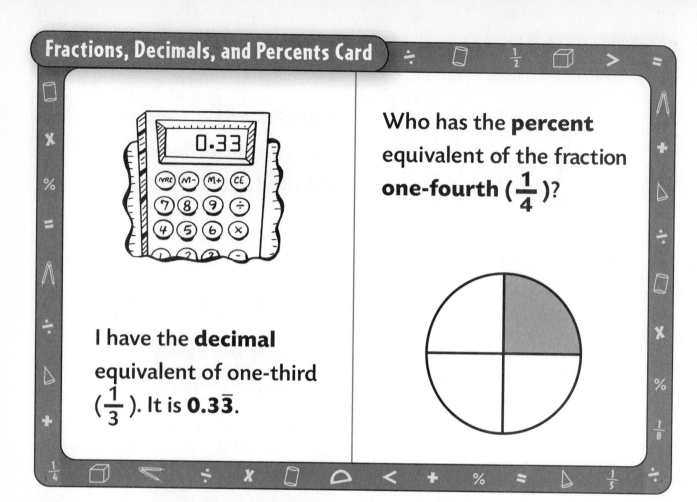

Fractions, Decimals, and Percents Card

I have the **decimal** equivalent of one-third ($\frac{1}{3}$). It is **0.3$\overline{3}$**.

Who has the **percent** equivalent of the fraction **one-fourth** ($\frac{1}{4}$)?

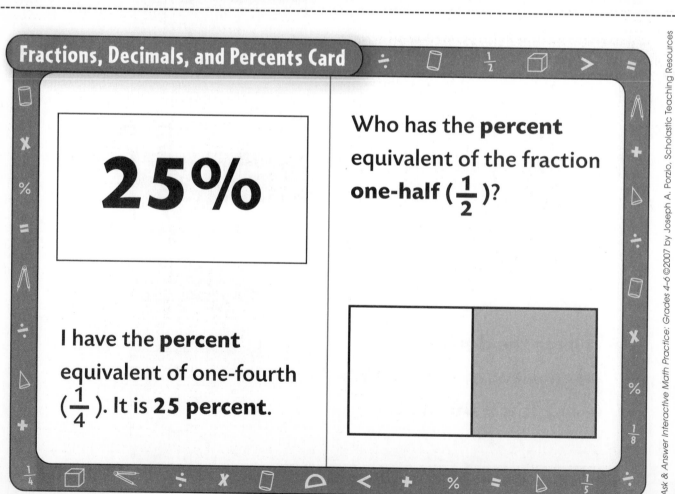

Fractions, Decimals, and Percents Card

25%

I have the **percent** equivalent of one-fourth ($\frac{1}{4}$). It is **25 percent**.

Who has the **percent** equivalent of the fraction **one-half** ($\frac{1}{2}$)?

Ask & Answer Interactive Math Practice: Grades 4–6 ©2007 by Joseph A. Porzio, Scholastic Teaching Resources

Fractions, Decimals, and Percents Card

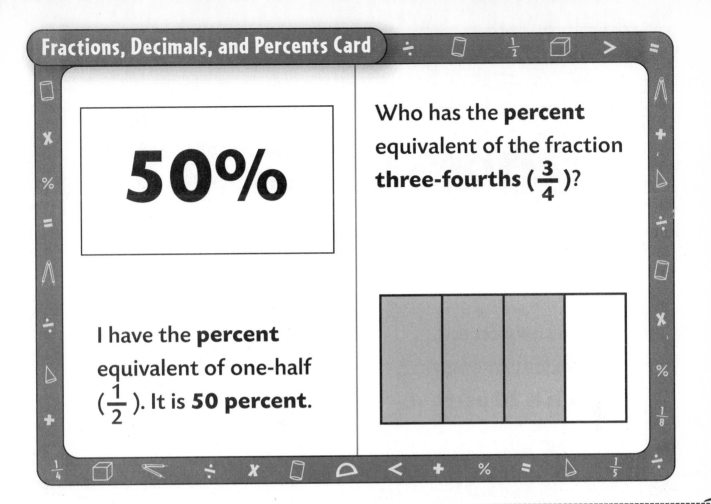

50%

Who has the **percent** equivalent of the fraction **three-fourths ($\frac{3}{4}$)?**

I have the **percent** equivalent of one-half ($\frac{1}{2}$). It is **50 percent**.

Fractions, Decimals, and Percents Card

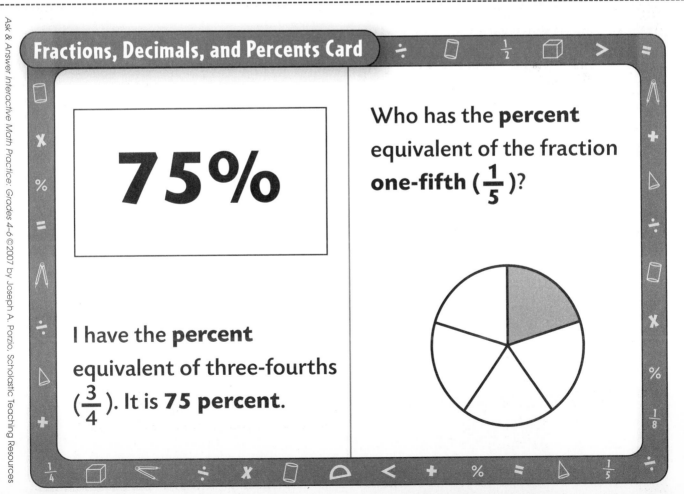

75%

Who has the **percent** equivalent of the fraction **one-fifth ($\frac{1}{5}$)?**

I have the **percent** equivalent of three-fourths ($\frac{3}{4}$). It is **75 percent**.

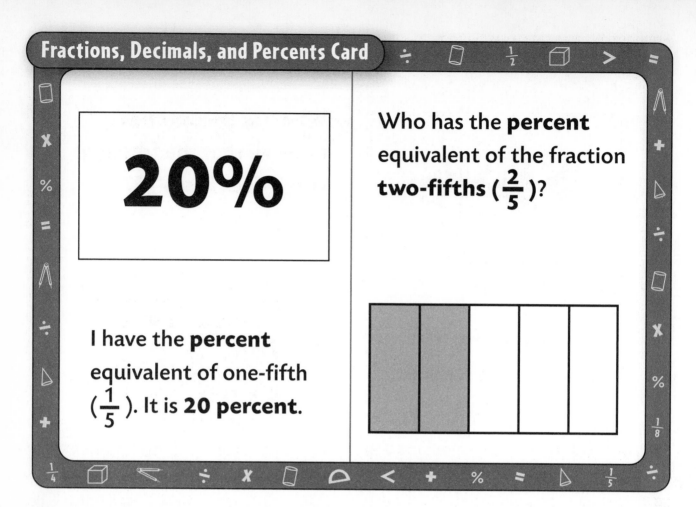

20%

Who has the **percent** equivalent of the fraction **two-fifths** ($\frac{2}{5}$)?

I have the **percent** equivalent of one-fifth ($\frac{1}{5}$). It is **20 percent**.

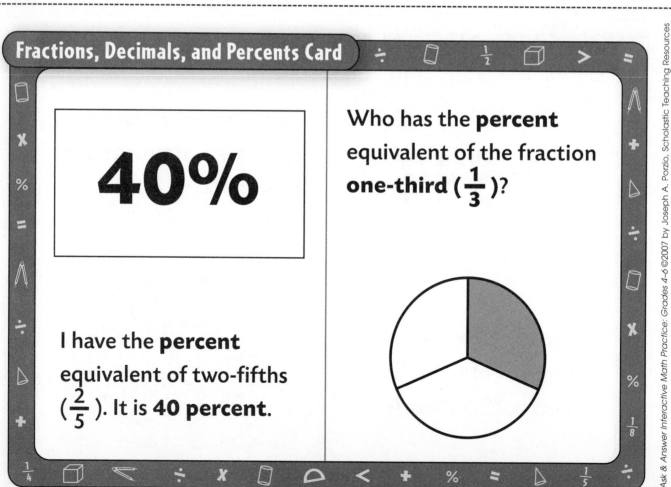

40%

Who has the **percent** equivalent of the fraction **one-third** ($\frac{1}{3}$)?

I have the **percent** equivalent of two-fifths ($\frac{2}{5}$). It is **40 percent**.

Ask & Answer Interactive Math Practice: Grades 4–6 ©2007 by Joseph A. Porzio, Scholastic Teaching Resources

Fractions, Decimals, and Percents Card

$$33\frac{1}{3}\%$$

I have the **percent** equivalent of one-third ($\frac{1}{3}$). It is **$33\frac{1}{3}$ percent**.

Who has the **fraction** equivalent of the decimal **three-tenths (0.3)**?

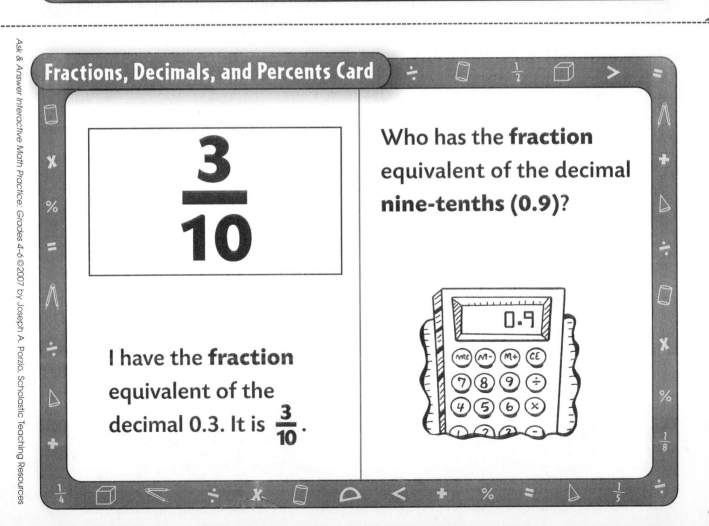

Fractions, Decimals, and Percents Card

$$\frac{3}{10}$$

I have the **fraction** equivalent of the decimal 0.3. It is $\frac{3}{10}$.

Who has the **fraction** equivalent of the decimal **nine-tenths (0.9)**?

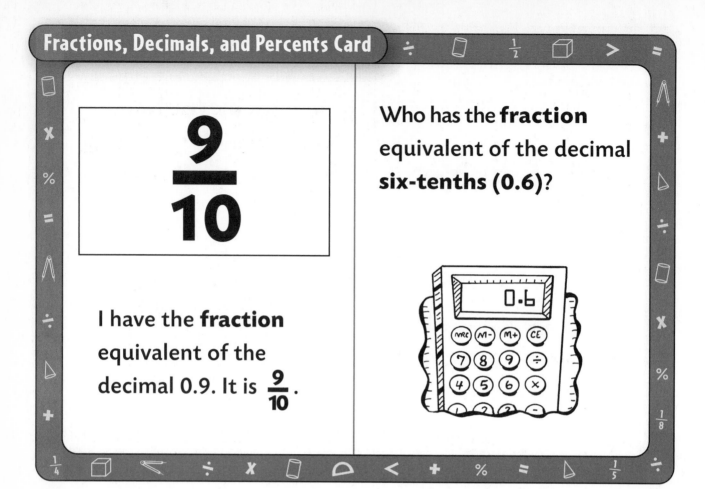

$$\frac{9}{10}$$

Who has the **fraction** equivalent of the decimal **six-tenths (0.6)**?

I have the **fraction** equivalent of the decimal 0.9. It is $\frac{9}{10}$.

Fractions, Decimals, and Percents Card

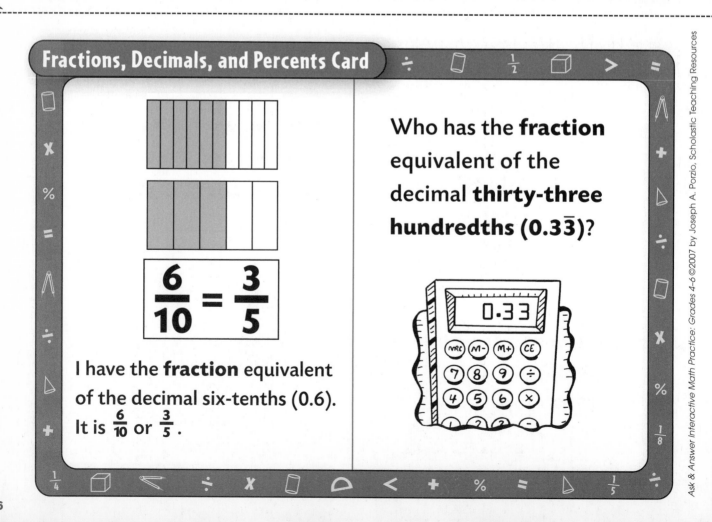

$$\frac{6}{10} = \frac{3}{5}$$

Who has the **fraction** equivalent of the decimal **thirty-three hundredths (0.3\bar{3})**?

I have the **fraction** equivalent of the decimal six-tenths (0.6). It is $\frac{6}{10}$ or $\frac{3}{5}$.

Ask & Answer Interactive Math Practice: Grades 4–6 ©2007 by Joseph A. Porzio, Scholastic Teaching Resources

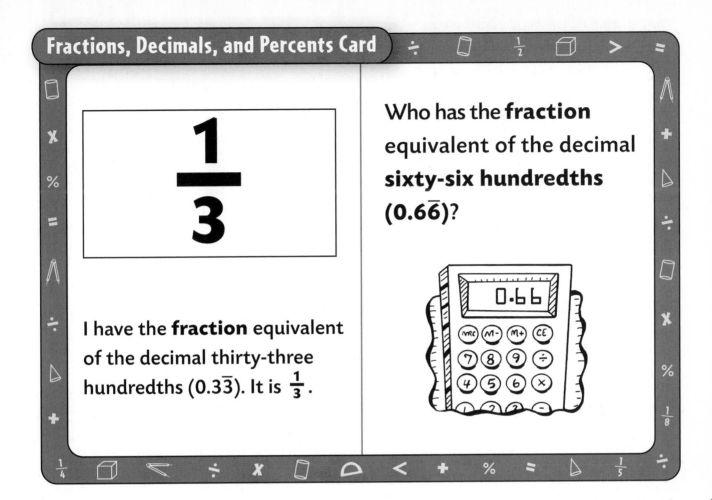

Fractions, Decimals, and Percents Card

$$\frac{1}{3}$$

I have the **fraction** equivalent of the decimal thirty-three hundredths (0.3$\overline{3}$). It is $\frac{1}{3}$.

Who has the **fraction** equivalent of the decimal **sixty-six hundredths (0.6$\overline{6}$)**?

0.66

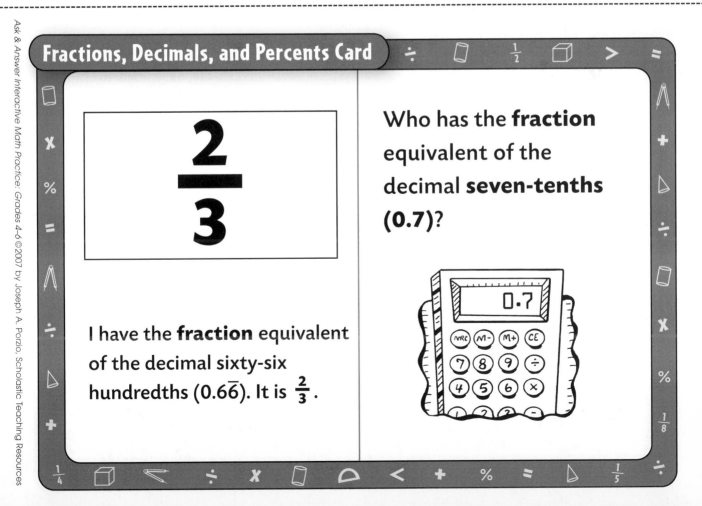

Fractions, Decimals, and Percents Card

$$\frac{2}{3}$$

I have the **fraction** equivalent of the decimal sixty-six hundredths (0.6$\overline{6}$). It is $\frac{2}{3}$.

Who has the **fraction** equivalent of the decimal **seven-tenths (0.7)**?

0.7

77

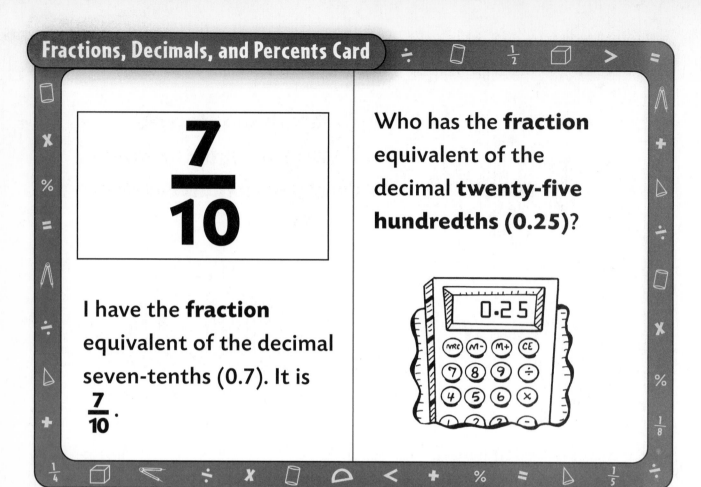

$$\frac{7}{10}$$

I have the **fraction** equivalent of the decimal seven-tenths (0.7). It is $\frac{7}{10}$.

Who has the **fraction** equivalent of the decimal **twenty-five hundredths (0.25)**?

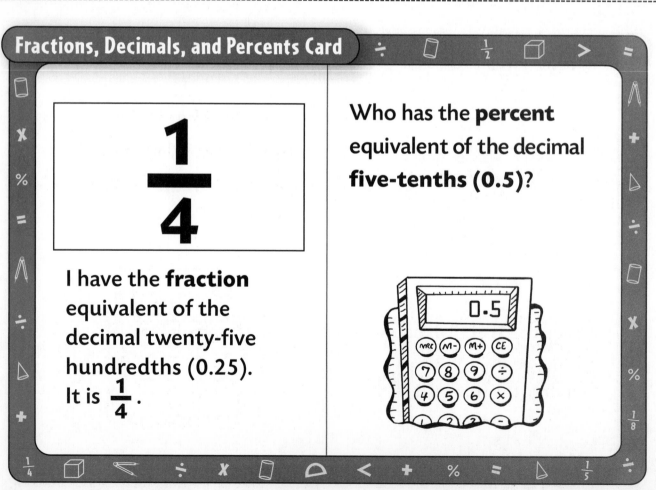

$$\frac{1}{4}$$

I have the **fraction** equivalent of the decimal twenty-five hundredths (0.25). It is $\frac{1}{4}$.

Who has the **percent** equivalent of the decimal **five-tenths (0.5)**?

Ask & Answer Interactive Math Practice: Grades 4–6 ©2007 by Joseph A. Porzio, Scholastic Teaching Resources

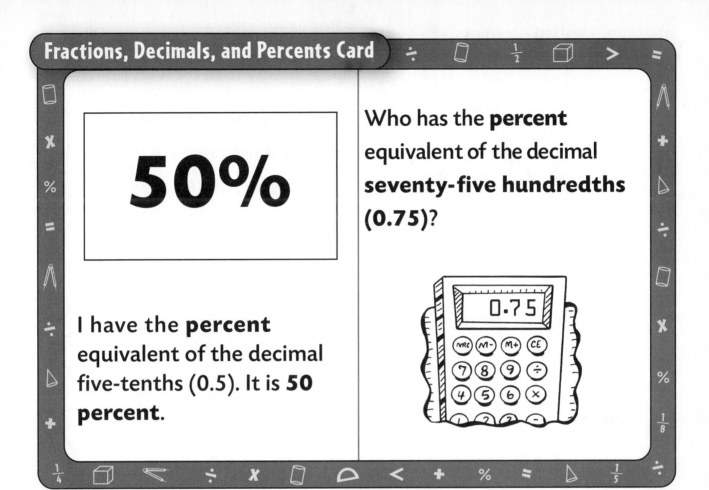

50%

I have the **percent** equivalent of the decimal five-tenths (0.5). It is **50 percent**.

Who has the **percent** equivalent of the decimal **seventy-five hundredths (0.75)?**

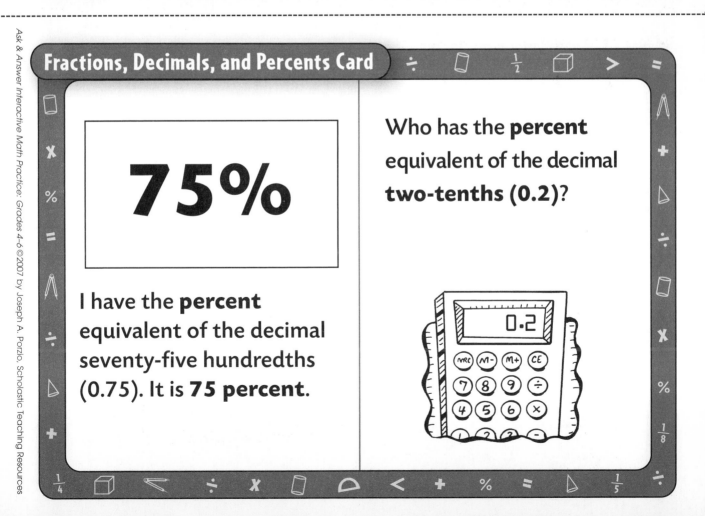

75%

I have the **percent** equivalent of the decimal seventy-five hundredths (0.75). It is **75 percent**.

Who has the **percent** equivalent of the decimal **two-tenths (0.2)?**

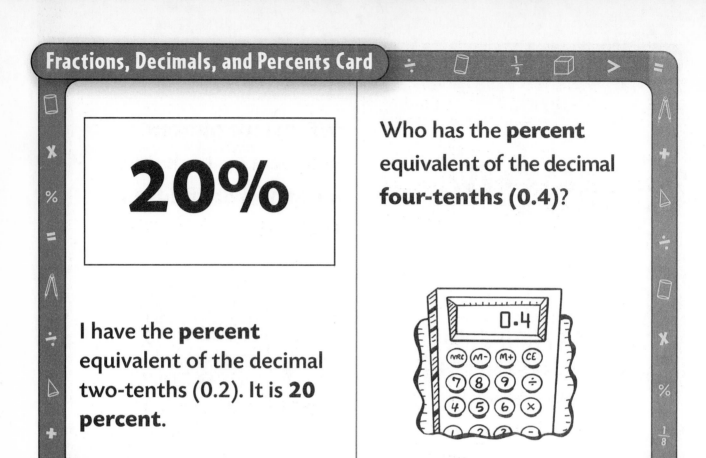

20%

I have the **percent** equivalent of the decimal two-tenths (0.2). It is **20 percent**.

Who has the **percent** equivalent of the decimal **four-tenths (0.4)**?

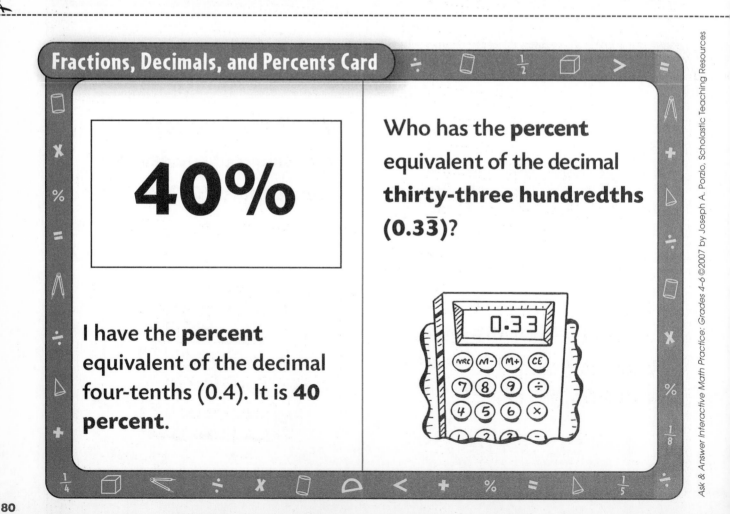

40%

I have the **percent** equivalent of the decimal four-tenths (0.4). It is **40 percent**.

Who has the **percent** equivalent of the decimal **thirty-three hundredths (0.3̄3̄)**?

Ask & Answer Interactive Math Practice: Grades 4–6 ©2007 by Joseph A. Porzio, Scholastic Teaching Resources

$33\frac{1}{3}\%$

I have the **percent** equivalent of the decimal thirty-three hundredths (0.3$\overline{3}$). It is **33$\frac{1}{3}$ percent**.

Who has the **percent** equivalent of the decimal **sixty-six hundredths (0.6$\overline{6}$)**?

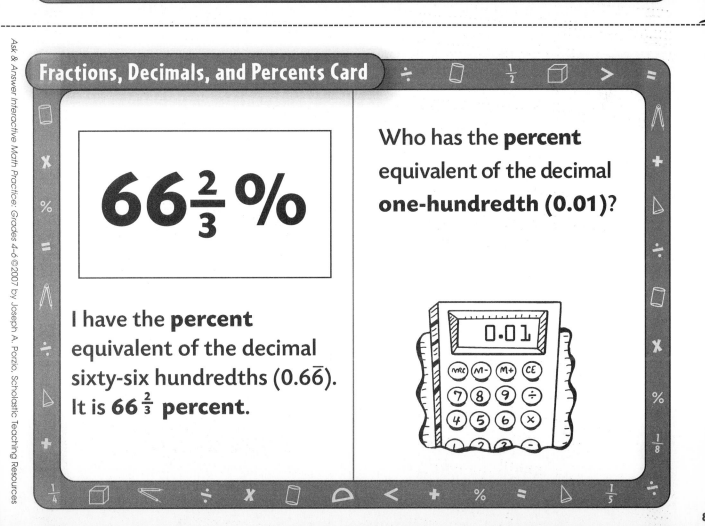

$66\frac{2}{3}\%$

I have the **percent** equivalent of the decimal sixty-six hundredths (0.6$\overline{6}$). It is **66$\frac{2}{3}$ percent**.

Who has the **percent** equivalent of the decimal **one-hundredth (0.01)**?

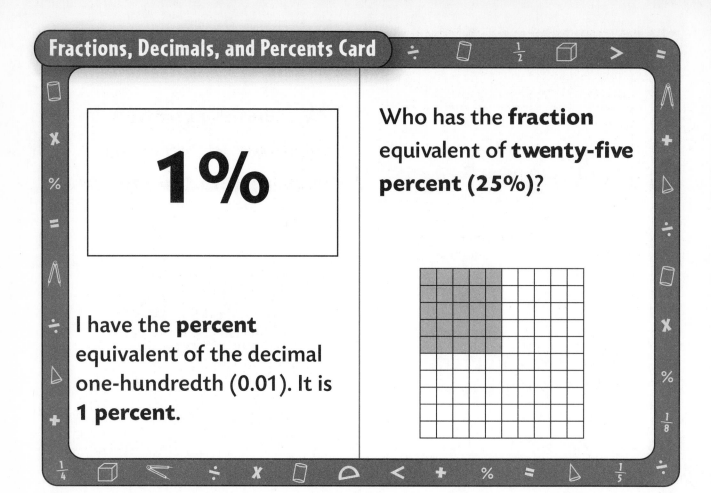

1%

Who has the **fraction** equivalent of **twenty-five percent (25%)**?

I have the **percent** equivalent of the decimal one-hundredth (0.01). It is **1 percent**.

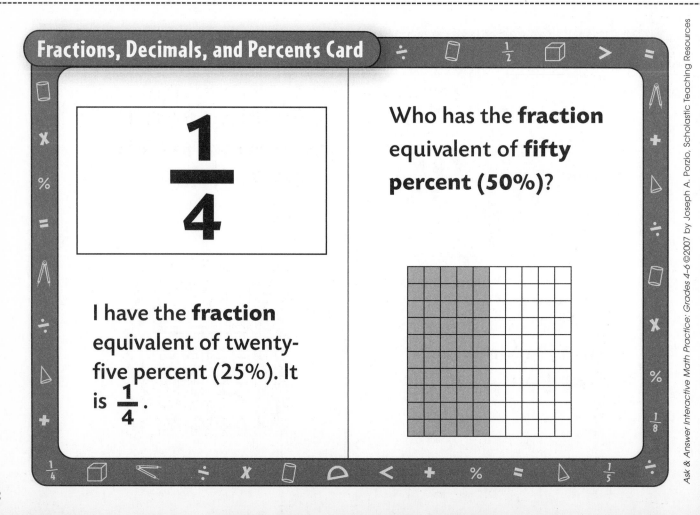

$\dfrac{1}{4}$

Who has the **fraction** equivalent of **fifty percent (50%)**?

I have the **fraction** equivalent of twenty-five percent (25%). It is $\dfrac{1}{4}$.

Ask & Answer Interactive Math Practice: Grades 4–6 ©2007 by Joseph A. Porzio, Scholastic Teaching Resources

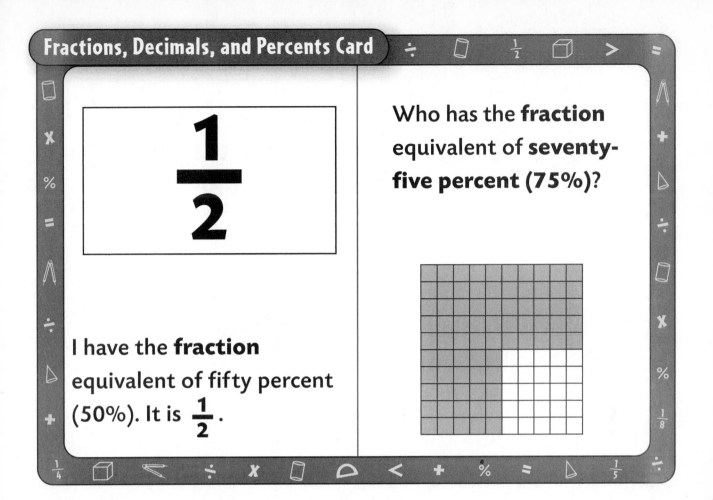

Fractions, Decimals, and Percents Card

$$\frac{1}{2}$$

Who has the **fraction** equivalent of **seventy-five percent (75%)**?

I have the **fraction** equivalent of fifty percent (50%). It is $\frac{1}{2}$.

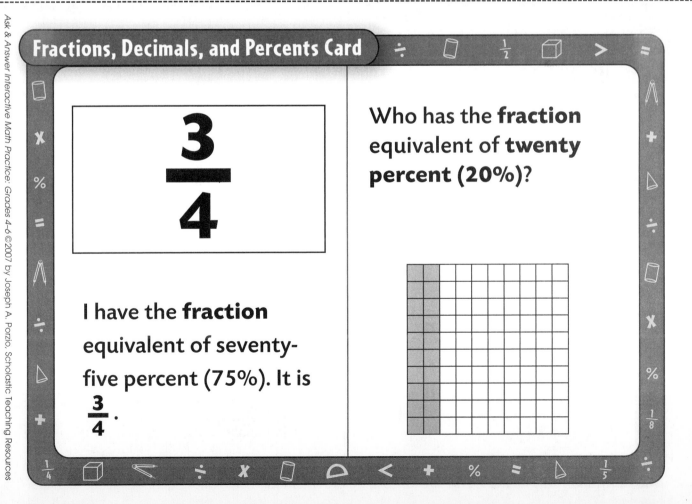

Fractions, Decimals, and Percents Card

$$\frac{3}{4}$$

Who has the **fraction** equivalent of **twenty percent (20%)**?

I have the **fraction** equivalent of seventy-five percent (75%). It is $\frac{3}{4}$.

$$\frac{1}{5}$$

I have the **fraction** equivalent of twenty percent (20%). It is $\frac{1}{5}$.

Who has the **fraction** equivalent of **forty percent (40%)**?

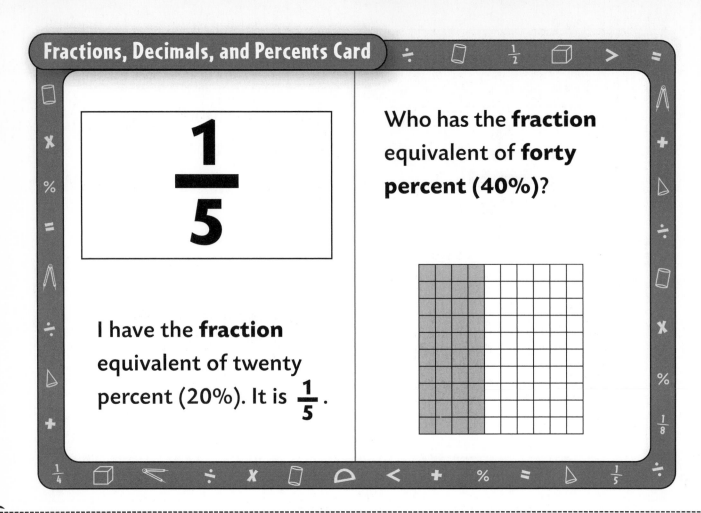

$$\frac{2}{5}$$

I have the **fraction** equivalent of forty percent (40%). It is $\frac{2}{5}$.

Who has the **fraction** equivalent of **thirty-three and one-third percent** $(33\frac{1}{3}\%)$?

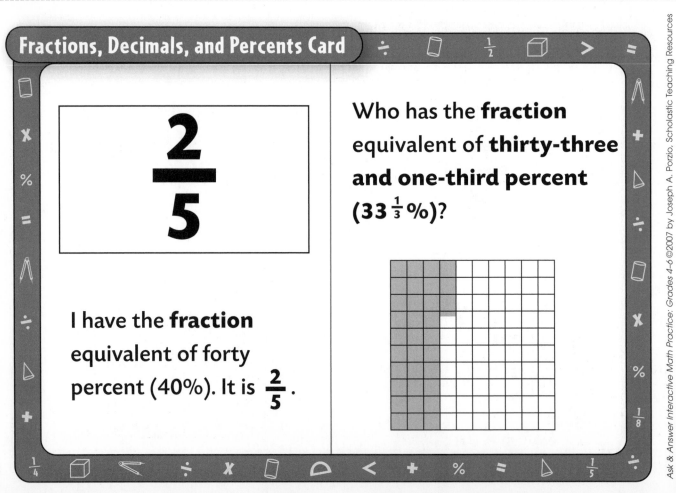

Ask & Answer Interactive Math Practice: Grades 4–6 ©2007 by Joseph A. Porzio, Scholastic Teaching Resources

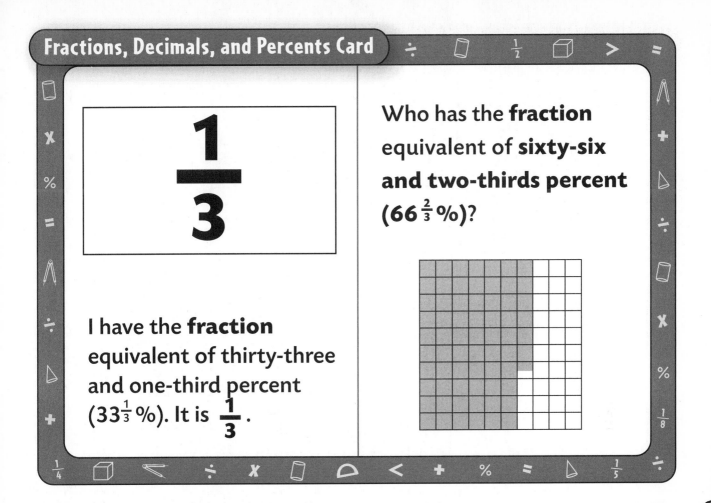

$$\frac{1}{3}$$

Who has the **fraction** equivalent of **sixty-six and two-thirds percent (66$\frac{2}{3}$%)**?

I have the **fraction** equivalent of thirty-three and one-third percent (33$\frac{1}{3}$%). It is $\frac{1}{3}$.

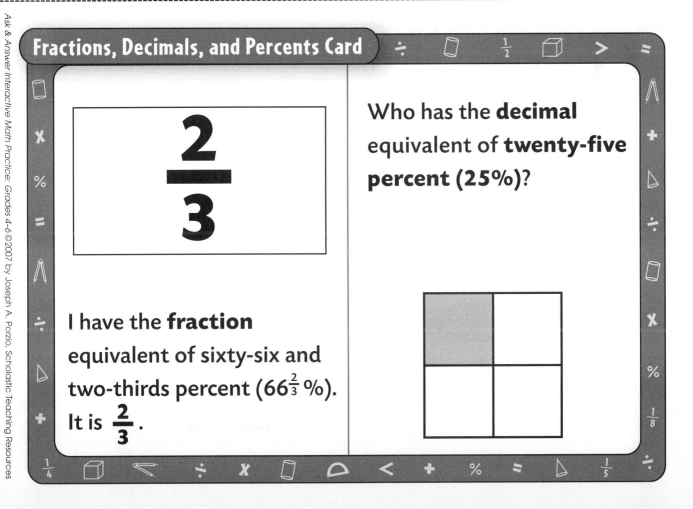

$$\frac{2}{3}$$

Who has the **decimal** equivalent of **twenty-five percent (25%)**?

I have the **fraction** equivalent of sixty-six and two-thirds percent (66$\frac{2}{3}$%). It is $\frac{2}{3}$.

Ask & Answer Interactive Math Practice: Grades 4–6 ©2007 by Joseph A. Porzio, Scholastic Teaching Resources

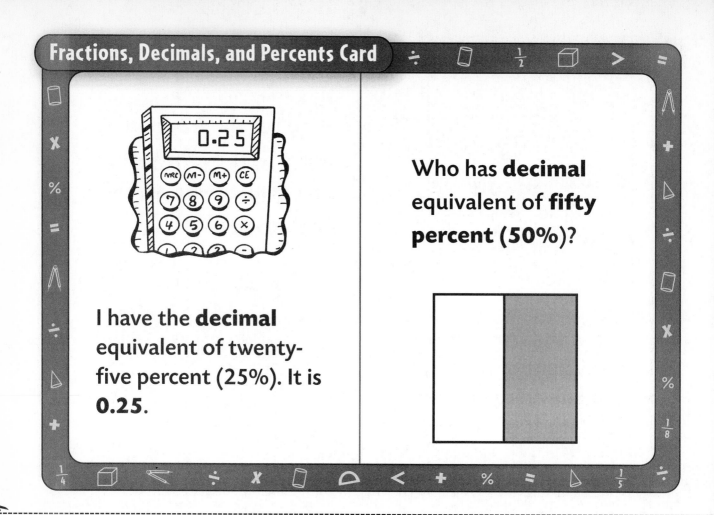

I have the **decimal** equivalent of twenty-five percent (25%). It is **0.25**.

Who has **decimal** equivalent of **fifty percent (50%)**?

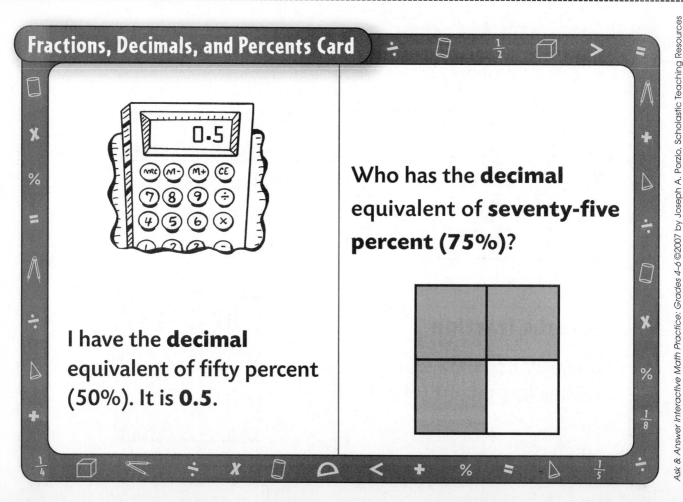

I have the **decimal** equivalent of fifty percent (50%). It is **0.5**.

Who has the **decimal** equivalent of **seventy-five percent (75%)**?

Ask & Answer Interactive Math Practice: Grades 4–6 ©2007 by Joseph A. Porzio, Scholastic Teaching Resources

Fractions, Decimals, and Percents Card

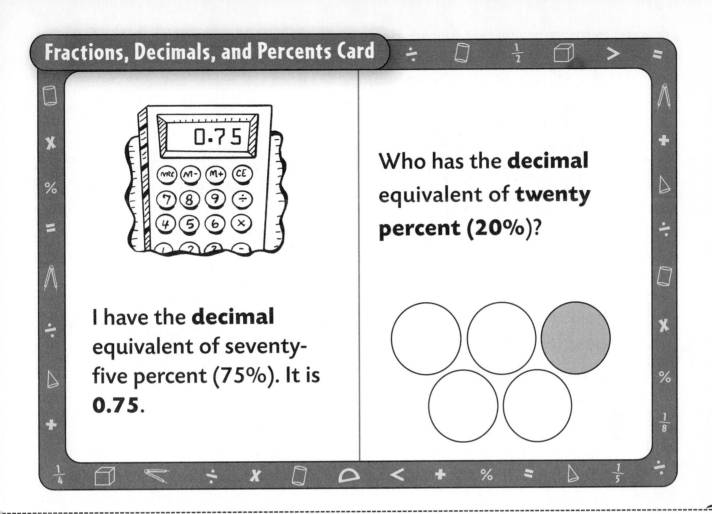

I have the **decimal** equivalent of seventy-five percent (75%). It is **0.75**.

Who has the **decimal** equivalent of **twenty percent (20%)**?

Fractions, Decimals, and Percents Card

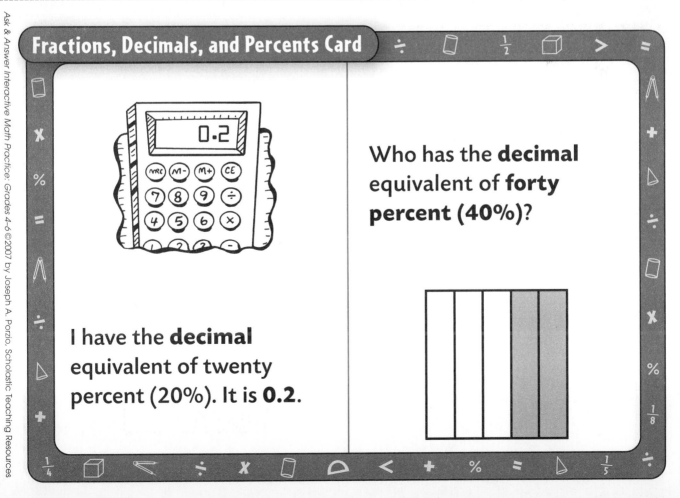

I have the **decimal** equivalent of twenty percent (20%). It is **0.2**.

Who has the **decimal** equivalent of **forty percent (40%)**?

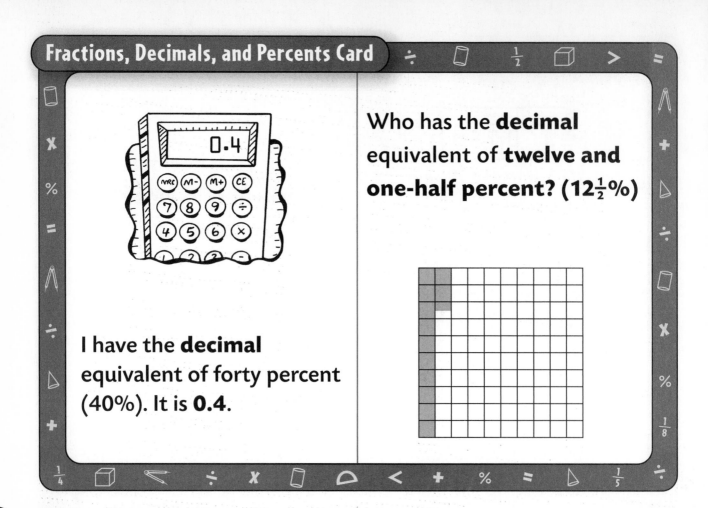

Who has the **decimal equivalent of twelve and one-half percent? ($12\frac{1}{2}$%)**

I have the **decimal** equivalent of forty percent (40%). It is **0.4**.

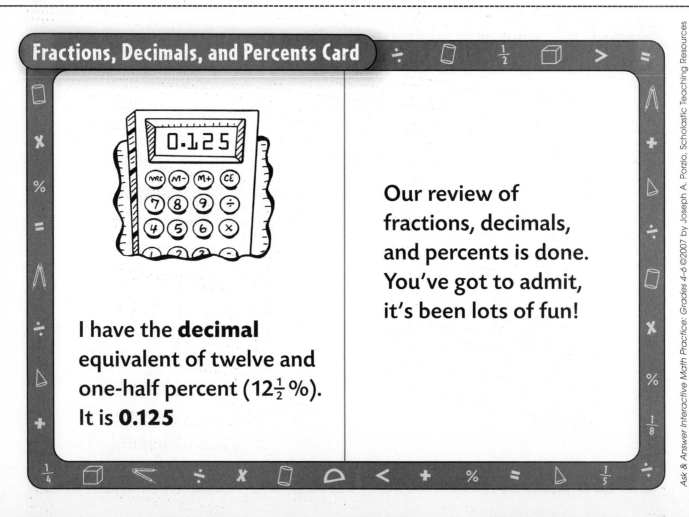

Our review of fractions, decimals, and percents is done. You've got to admit, it's been lots of fun!

I have the **decimal** equivalent of twelve and one-half percent ($12\frac{1}{2}$%). It is **0.125**

Ask & Answer Interactive Math Practice: Grades 4–6 ©2007 by Joseph A. Porzio, Scholastic Teaching Resources

And now for our enlightenment, We'll review **geometry and measurement**.

Who has the **regular polygon** with four equal sides and all angles equal to 90 degrees (90°)?

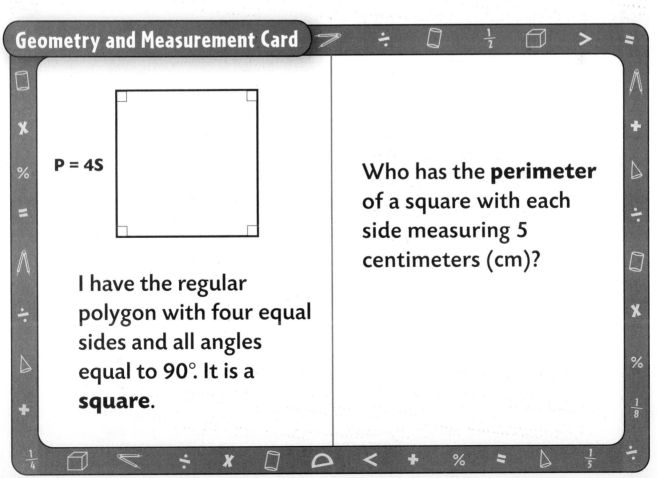

P = 4S

I have the regular polygon with four equal sides and all angles equal to 90°. It is a **square**.

Who has the **perimeter** of a square with each side measuring 5 centimeters (cm)?

P = 4S

5 cm

I have the perimeter of a square with each side measuring 5 centimeters. It is **20 centimeters**.

Who has the **regular polygon** that has three equal sides and three equal angles?

I have the regular polygon that has three equal sides and three equal angles. It is an **equilateral triangle**.

Who has the **perimeter** of an equilateral triangle with each side measuring 7 centimeters?

Ask & Answer Interactive Math Practice: Grades 4–6 ©2007 by Joseph A. Porzio, Scholastic Teaching Resources

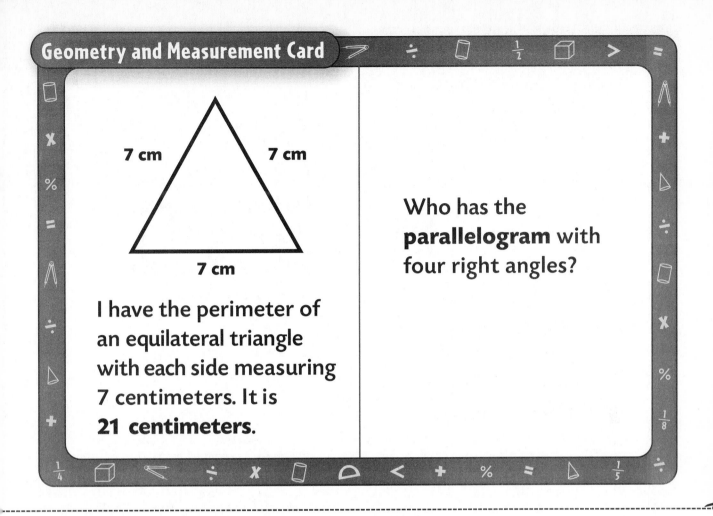

7 cm   **7 cm**

7 cm

I have the perimeter of an equilateral triangle with each side measuring 7 centimeters. It is **21 centimeters**.

Who has the **parallelogram** with four right angles?

Ask & Answer Interactive Math Practice: Grades 4–6 ©2007 by Joseph A. Porzio, Scholastic Teaching Resources

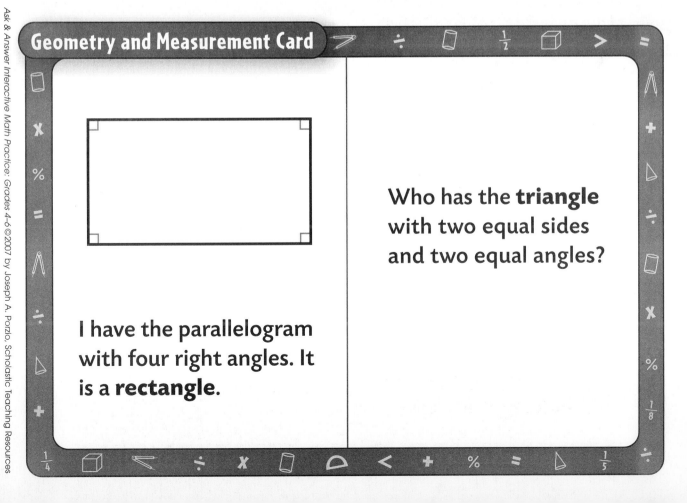

I have the parallelogram with four right angles. It is a **rectangle**.

Who has the **triangle** with two equal sides and two equal angles?

45°   45°

I have the triangle with two equal sides and two equal angles. It is an **isosceles triangle**.

Who has the **triangle** with sides of different lengths and no angles the same?

---

9 cm   7 cm

12 cm

I have the triangle with sides of different lengths and no angles the same. It is a **scalene triangle**.

Who has the model of a **cube** and knows how many faces it has?

Ask & Answer Interactive Math Practice: Grades 4–6 ©2007 by Joseph A. Porzio, Scholastic Teaching Resources

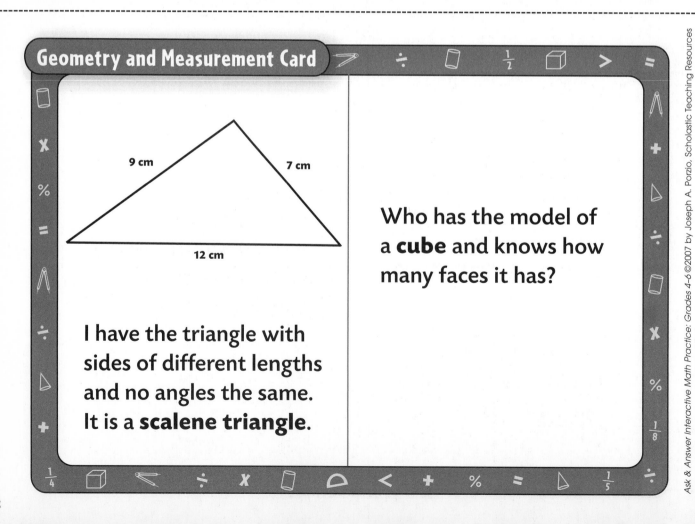

Geometry and Measurement Card

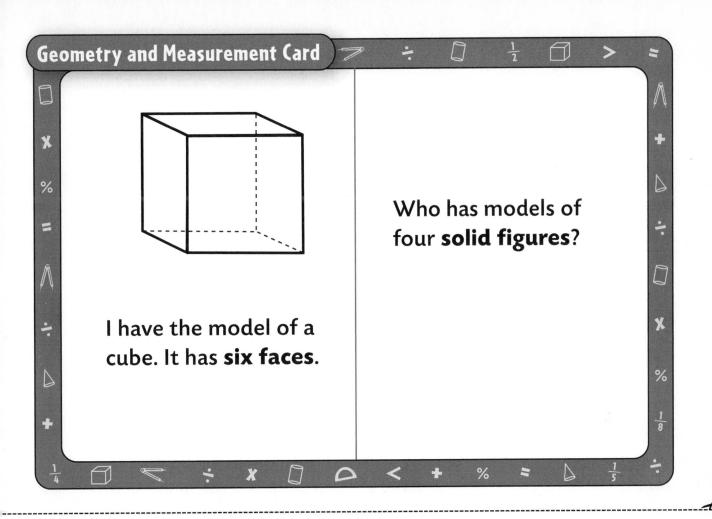

Who has models of four **solid figures**?

I have the model of a cube. It has **six faces**.

Geometry and Measurement Card

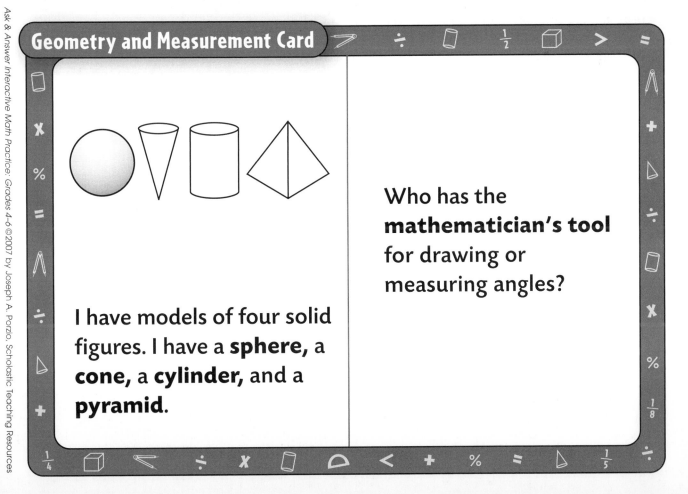

Who has the **mathematician's tool** for drawing or measuring angles?

I have models of four solid figures. I have a **sphere,** a **cone,** a **cylinder,** and a **pyramid**.

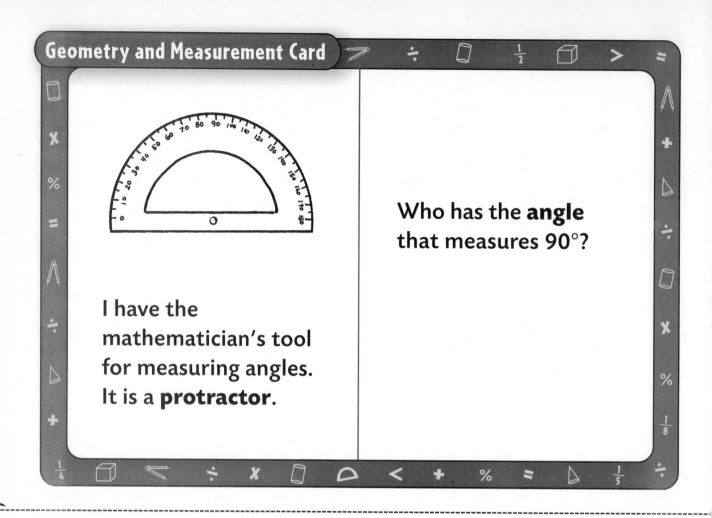

Who has the **angle** that measures 90°?

I have the mathematician's tool for measuring angles. It is a **protractor**.

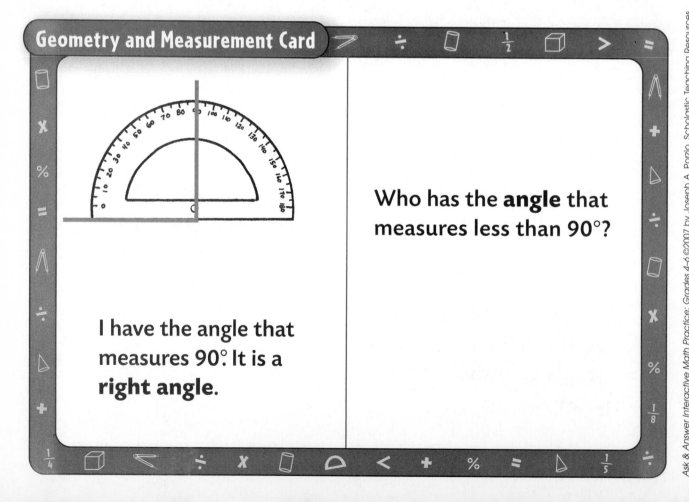

Who has the **angle** that measures less than 90°?

I have the angle that measures 90°. It is a **right angle**.

Ask & Answer Interactive Math Practice: Grades 4–6 ©2007 by Joseph A. Porzio, Scholastic Teaching Resources

Ask & Answer Interactive Math Practice: Grades 4–6 ©2007 by Joseph A. Porzio. Scholastic Teaching Resources

Geometry and Measurement Card

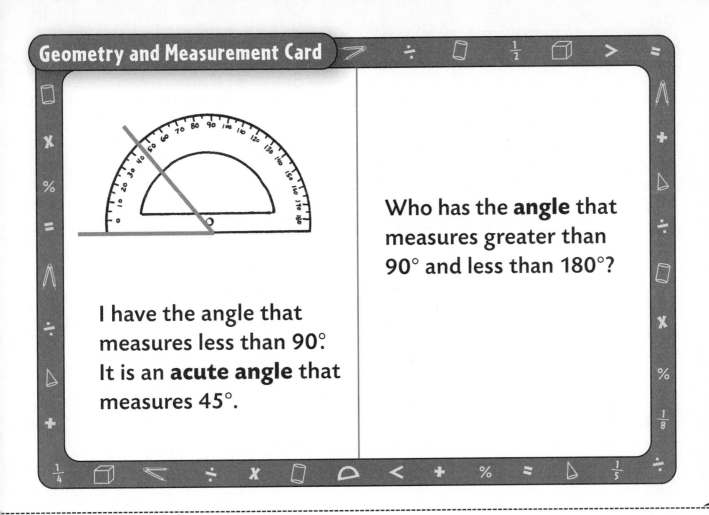

I have the angle that measures less than 90°. It is an **acute angle** that measures 45°.

Who has the **angle** that measures greater than 90° and less than 180°?

Geometry and Measurement Card

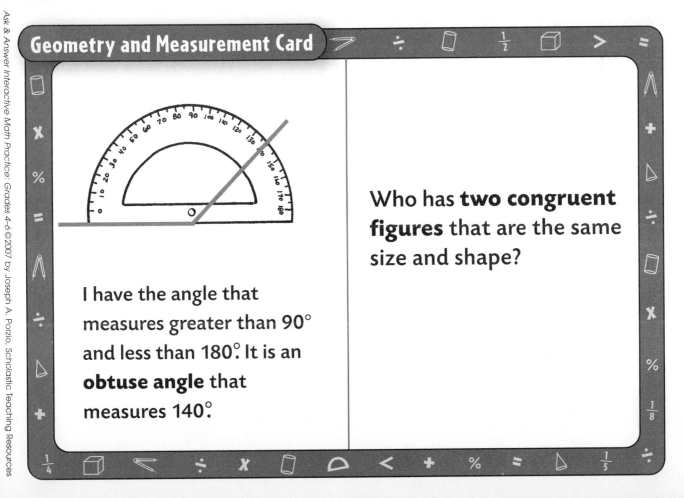

I have the angle that measures greater than 90° and less than 180°. It is an **obtuse angle** that measures 140°.

Who has **two congruent figures** that are the same size and shape?

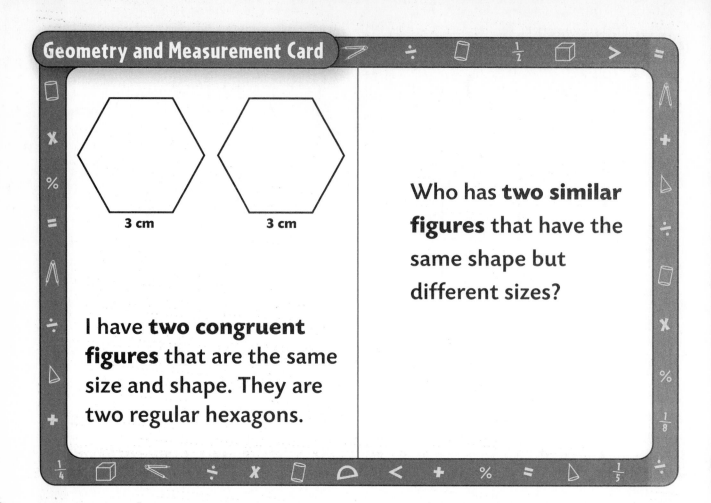

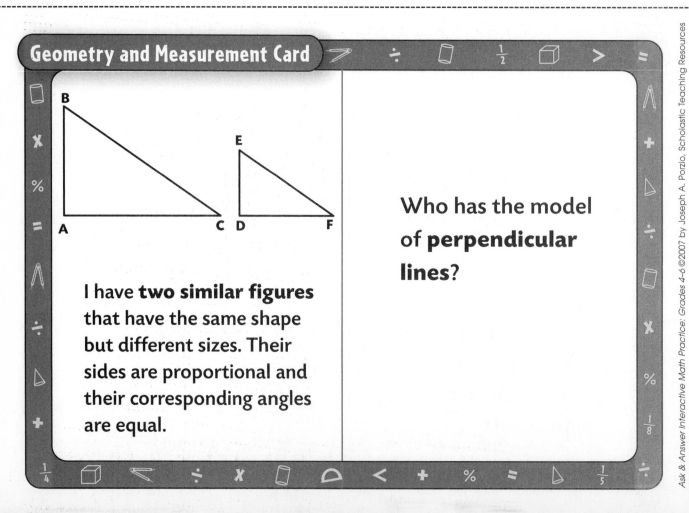

Ask & Answer Interactive Math Practice: Grades 4–6 ©2007 by Joseph A. Porzio, Scholastic Teaching Resources

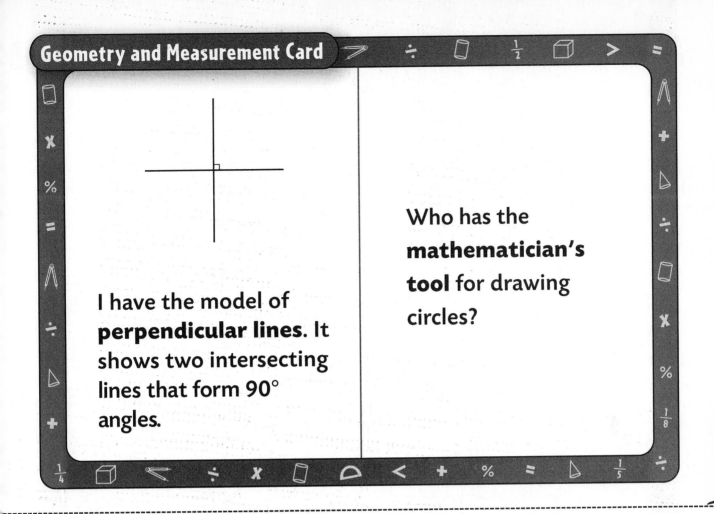

I have the model of **perpendicular lines**. It shows two intersecting lines that form 90° angles.

Who has the **mathematician's tool** for drawing circles?

Ask & Answer Interactive Math Practice: Grades 4–6 ©2007 by Joseph A. Porzio, Scholastic Teaching Resources

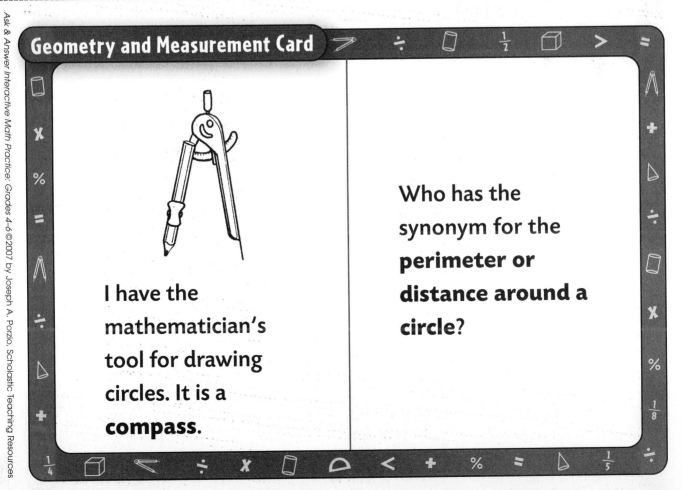

I have the mathematician's tool for drawing circles. It is a **compass**.

Who has the synonym for the **perimeter or distance around a circle**?

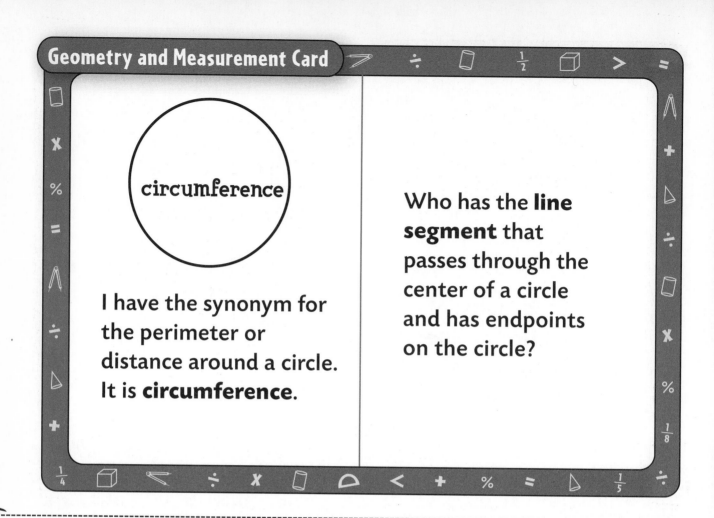

circumference

I have the synonym for the perimeter or distance around a circle. It is **circumference**.

Who has the **line segment** that passes through the center of a circle and has endpoints on the circle?

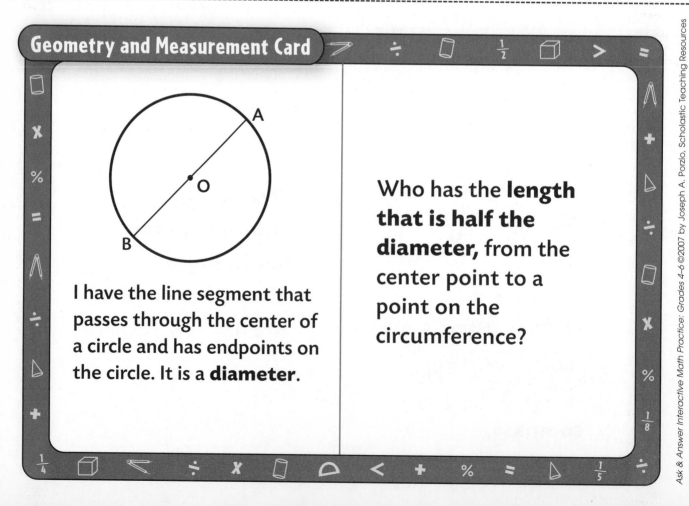

I have the line segment that passes through the center of a circle and has endpoints on the circle. It is a **diameter**.

Who has the **length that is half the diameter,** from the center point to a point on the circumference?

Ask & Answer Interactive Math Practice: Grades 4–6 ©2007 by Joseph A. Porzio, Scholastic Teaching Resources

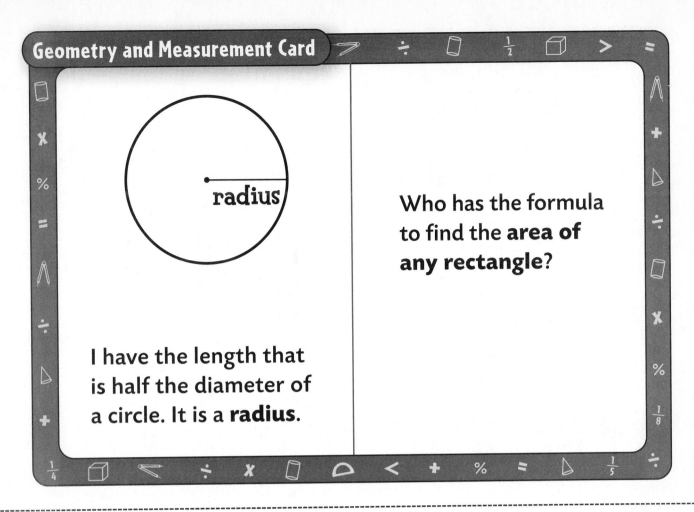

radius

Who has the formula to find the **area of any rectangle**?

I have the length that is half the diameter of a circle. It is a **radius**.

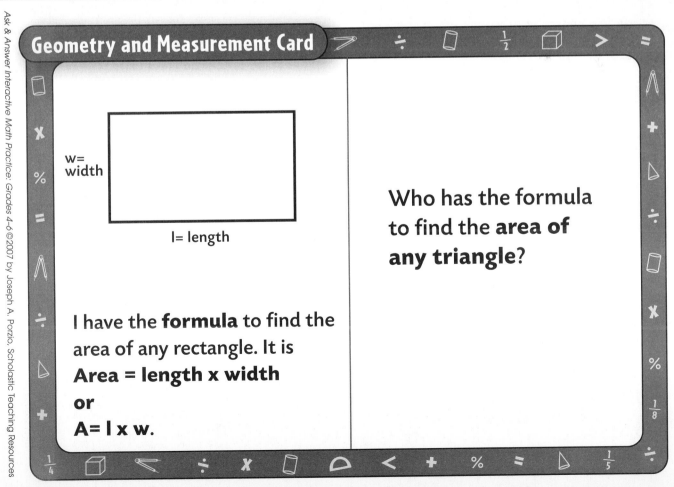

w= width

l= length

Who has the formula to find the **area of any triangle**?

I have the **formula** to find the area of any rectangle. It is
Area = length x width
or
A= l x w.

Ask & Answer Interactive Math Practice: Grades 4–6 © 2007 by Joseph A. Porzio, Scholastic Teaching Resources

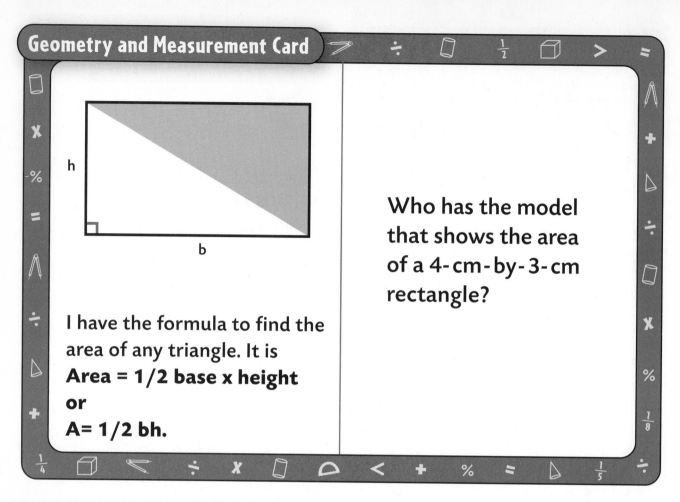

I have the formula to find the area of any triangle. It is
Area = 1/2 base x height
or
A= 1/2 bh.

Who has the model that shows the area of a 4-cm-by-3-cm rectangle?

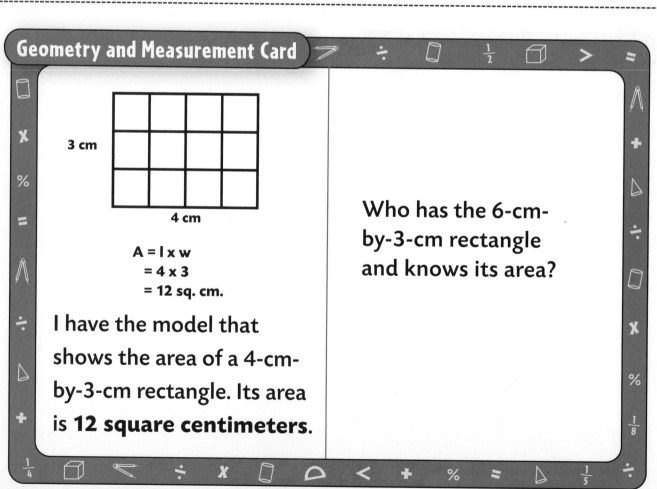

$A = l \times w$
$= 4 \times 3$
$= 12$ sq. cm.

I have the model that shows the area of a 4-cm-by-3-cm rectangle. Its area is **12 square centimeters**.

Who has the 6-cm-by-3-cm rectangle and knows its area?

Ask & Answer Interactive Math Practice: Grades 4–6 ©2007 by Joseph A. Porzio, Scholastic Teaching Resources

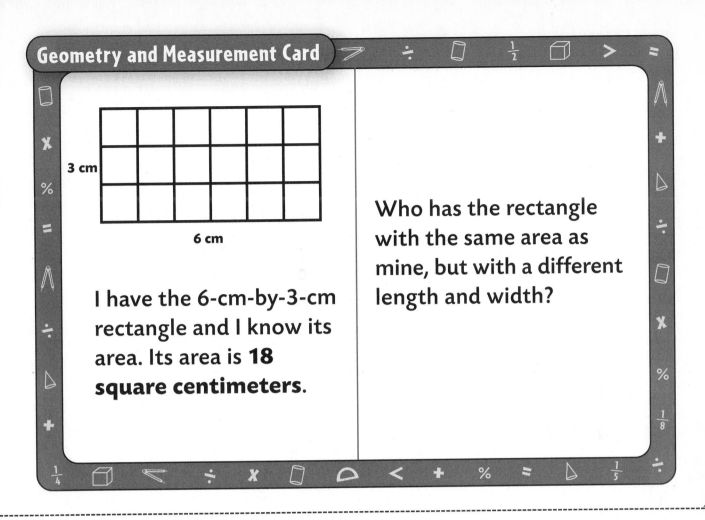

3 cm

6 cm

I have the 6-cm-by-3-cm rectangle and I know its area. Its area is **18 square centimeters**.

Who has the rectangle with the same area as mine, but with a different length and width?

Ask & Answer Interactive Math Practice: Grades 4–6 © 2007 by Joseph A. Porzio, Scholastic Teaching Resources

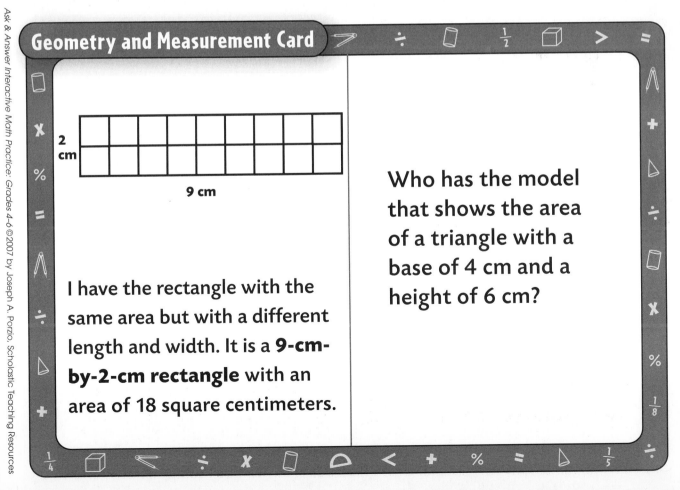

2 cm

9 cm

I have the rectangle with the same area but with a different length and width. It is a **9-cm-by-2-cm rectangle** with an area of 18 square centimeters.

Who has the model that shows the area of a triangle with a base of 4 cm and a height of 6 cm?

A = 1/2 bh
= 1/2 (4 x 6)
= 12 sq. cm.

h= 6 cm

b= 4 cm

I have the model that shows the area of a triangle with a base of 4 cm and a height of 6 cm. It is **12 square centimeters**.

Who has the triangle with a base of 5 cm and a height of 8 cm and knows its area?

A = 1/2 (5 x 8) = 20 sq. cm.

h= 8 cm

b= 5cm

I have the triangle with a base of 5 cm and a height of 8 cm. Its area is **20 square centimeters**.

Who has the **instrument** for measuring temperature?

Ask & Answer Interactive Math Practice: Grades 4–6 ©2007 by Joseph A. Porzio, Scholastic Teaching Resources

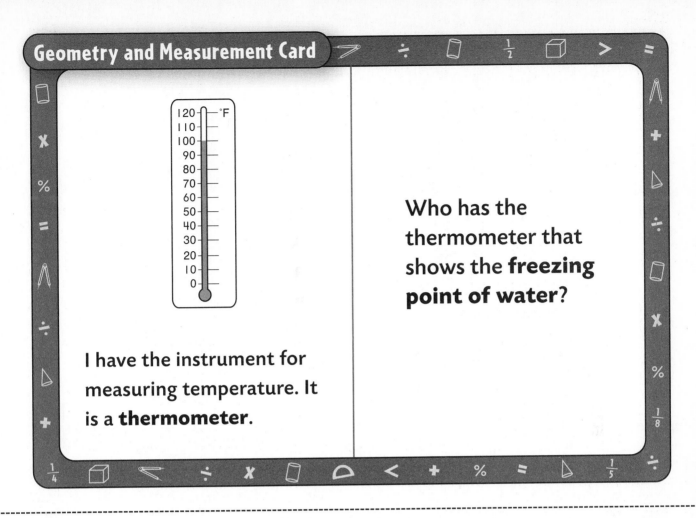

I have the instrument for measuring temperature. It is a **thermometer**.

Who has the thermometer that shows the **freezing point of water**?

Ask & Answer Interactive Math Practice: Grades 4–6 ©2007 by Joseph A. Porzio, Scholastic Teaching Resources

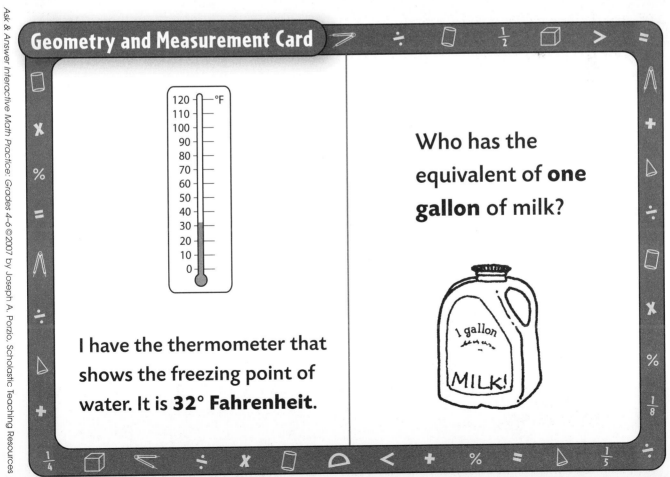

I have the thermometer that shows the freezing point of water. It is **32° Fahrenheit**.

Who has the equivalent of **one gallon** of milk?

I have the equivalent of one gallon of milk. It is **4 quarts** of milk.

Who has the equivalent of **one quart** of milk?

I have the equivalent of one quart of milk. It is **4 cups of milk**.

Who has the equivalent of **one liter** of juice?

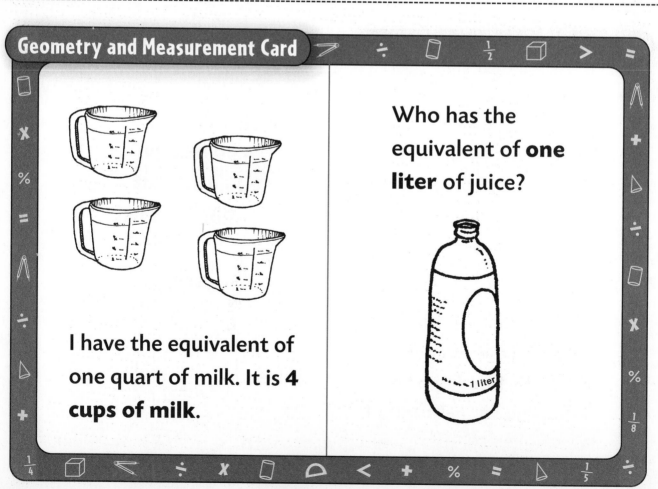

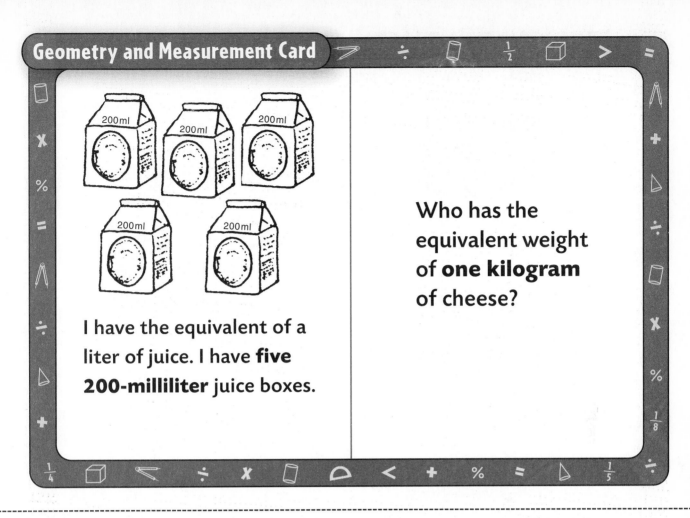

I have the equivalent of a liter of juice. I have **five 200-milliliter** juice boxes.

Who has the equivalent weight of **one kilogram** of cheese?

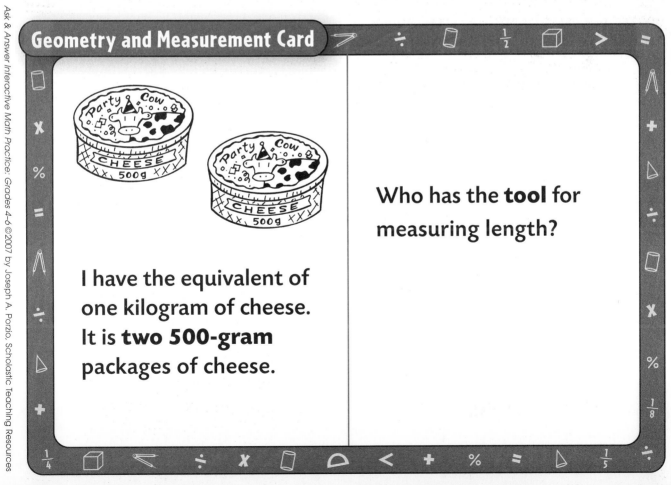

I have the equivalent of one kilogram of cheese. It is **two 500-gram** packages of cheese.

Who has the **tool** for measuring length?

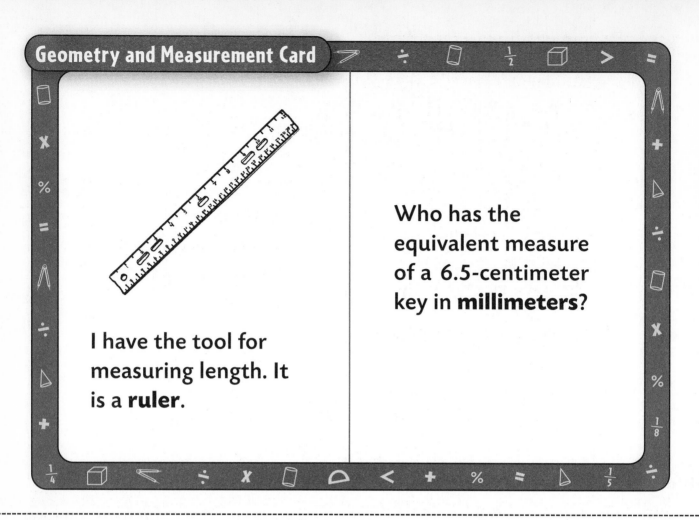

I have the tool for measuring length. It is a **ruler**.

Who has the equivalent measure of a 6.5-centimeter key in **millimeters**?

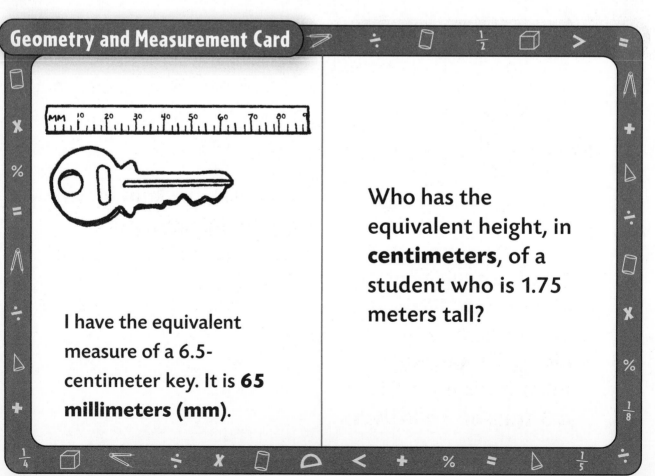

I have the equivalent measure of a 6.5-centimeter key. It is **65 millimeters (mm)**.

Who has the equivalent height, in **centimeters**, of a student who is 1.75 meters tall?

Ask & Answer Interactive Math Practice: Grades 4–6 ©2007 by Joseph A. Porzio. Scholastic Teaching Resources

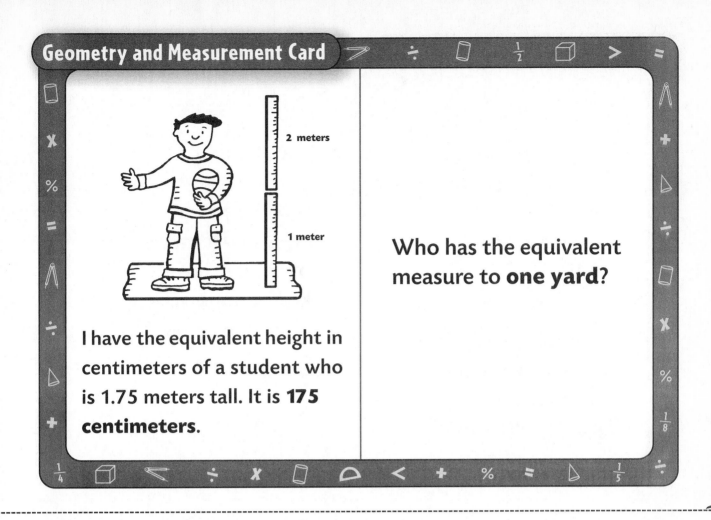

I have the equivalent height in centimeters of a student who is 1.75 meters tall. It is **175 centimeters**.

Who has the equivalent measure to **one yard**?

2 meters

1 meter

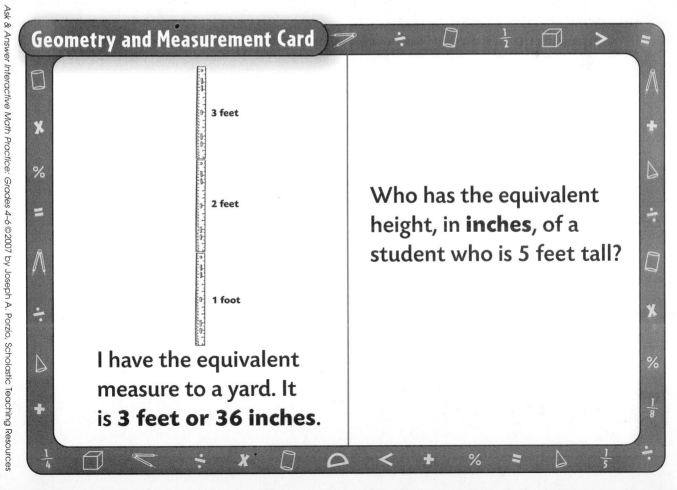

3 feet

2 feet

1 foot

I have the equivalent measure to a yard. It is **3 feet or 36 inches**.

Who has the equivalent height, in **inches**, of a student who is 5 feet tall?

I have the equivalent height, in inches, of a student who is 5 feet tall. It is **60 inches**.

Who has the equivalent, in **ounces**, of a one-pound box of chocolates?

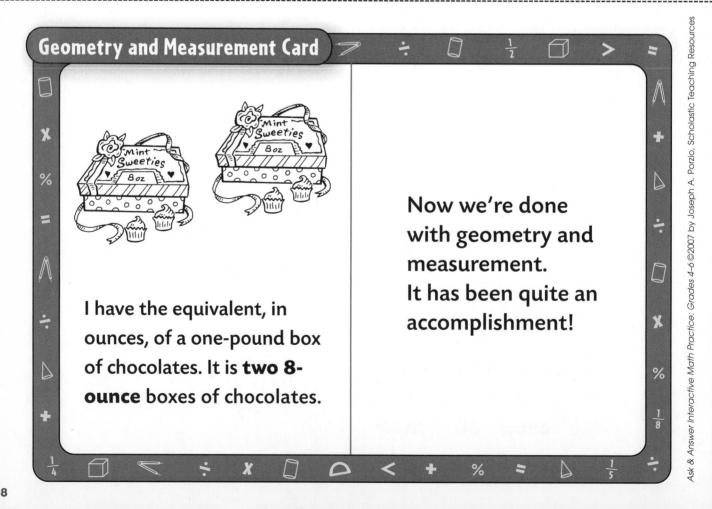

I have the equivalent, in ounces, of a one-pound box of chocolates. It is **two 8-ounce** boxes of chocolates.

Now we're done with geometry and measurement. It has been quite an accomplishment!

Ask & Answer Interactive Math Practice: Grades 4–6 ©2007 by Joseph A. Porzio, Scholastic Teaching Resources

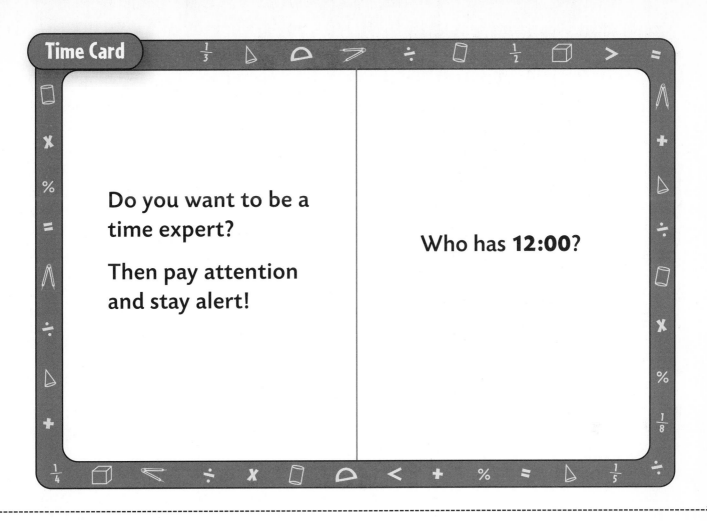

Do you want to be a time expert?

Then pay attention and stay alert!

Who has **12:00**?

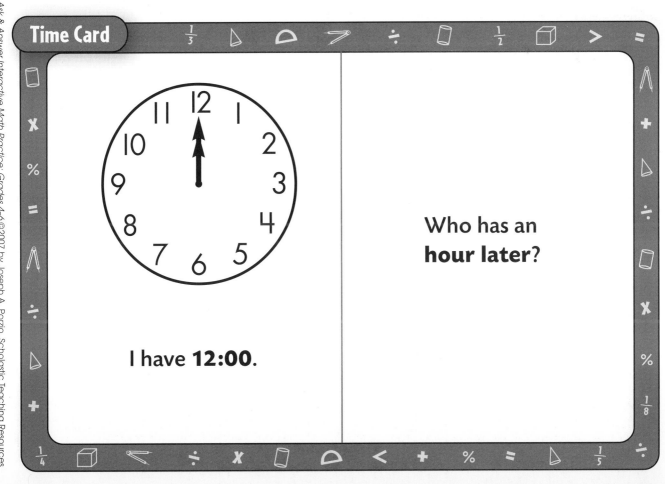

Who has an **hour later**?

I have **12:00**.

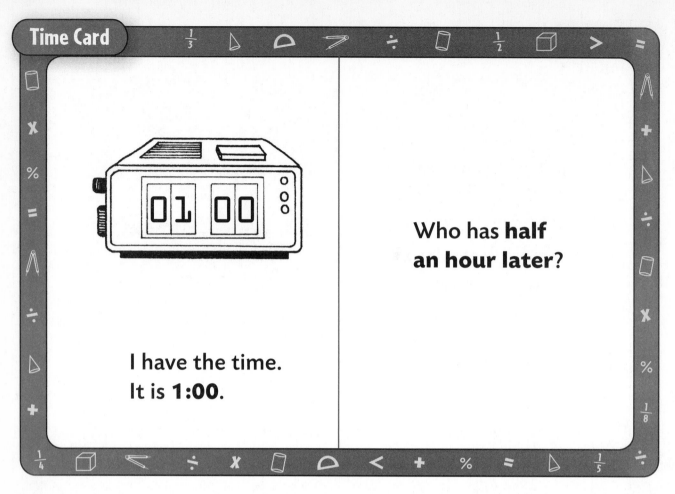

I have the time.
It is **1:00**.

Who has **half
an hour later**?

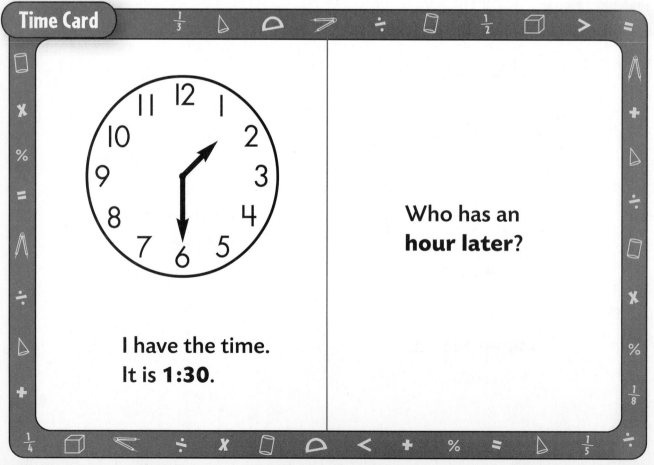

I have the time.
It is **1:30**.

Who has an
hour later?

Ask & Answer Interactive Math Practice: Grades 4–6 ©2007 by Joseph A. Porzio. Scholastic Teaching Resources

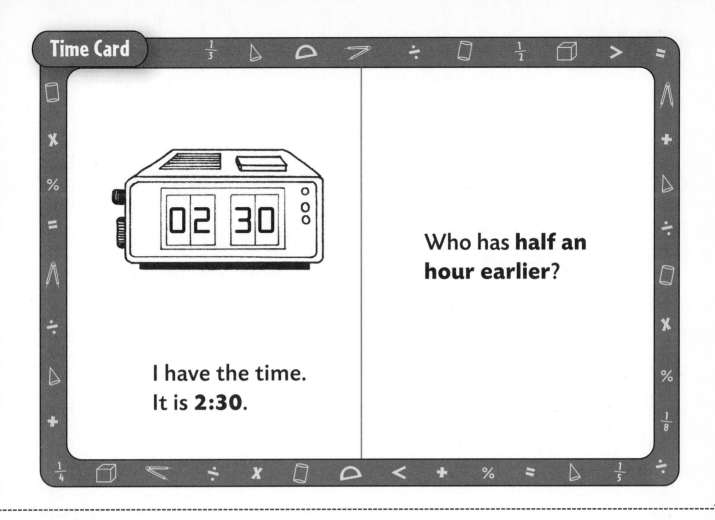

Time Card

I have the time. It is **2:30**.

Who has **half an hour earlier**?

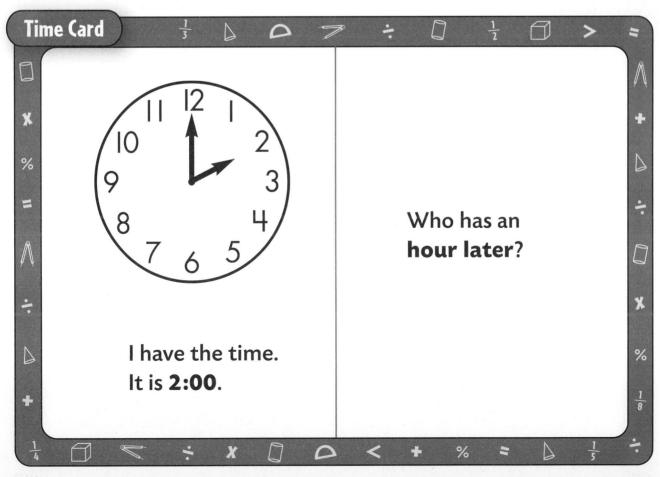

Time Card

I have the time. It is **2:00**.

Who has an **hour later**?

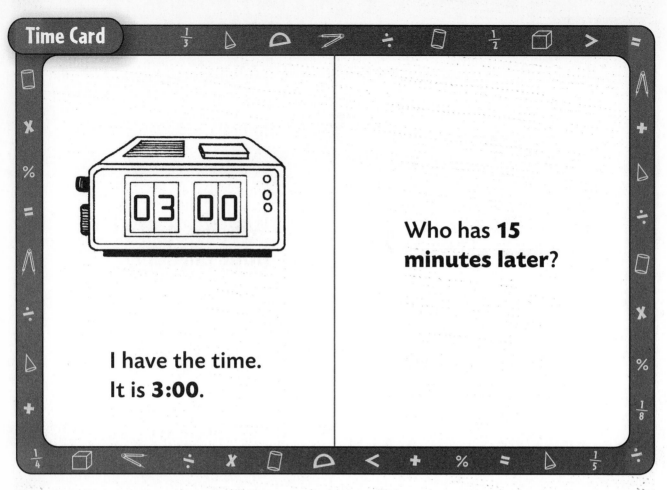

I have the time.
It is **3:00**.

Who has **15 minutes later**?

Time Card

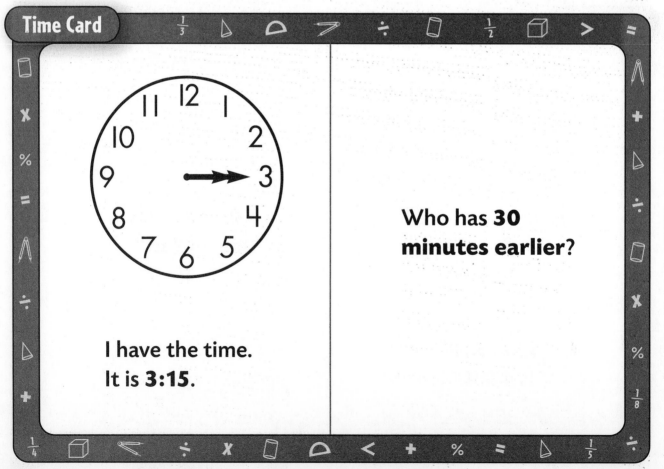

I have the time.
It is **3:15**.

Who has **30 minutes earlier**?

Ask & Answer Interactive Math Practice: Grades 4–6 ©2007 by Joseph A. Porzio, Scholastic Teaching Resources

I have the time.
It is **2:45**.

Who has an
hour later?

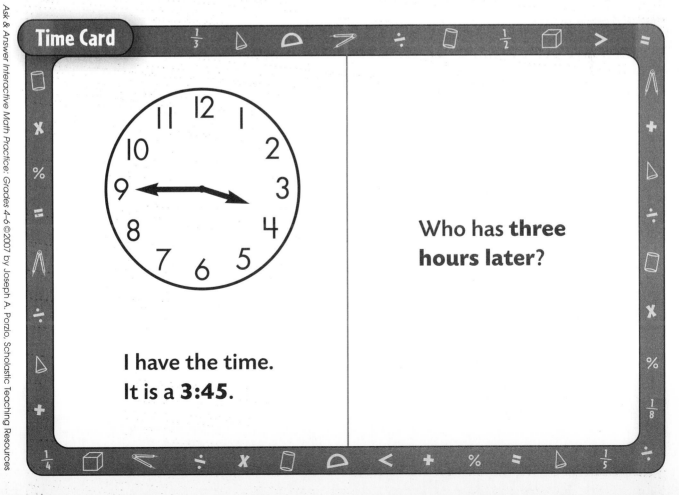

I have the time.
It is a **3:45**.

Who has **three
hours later?**

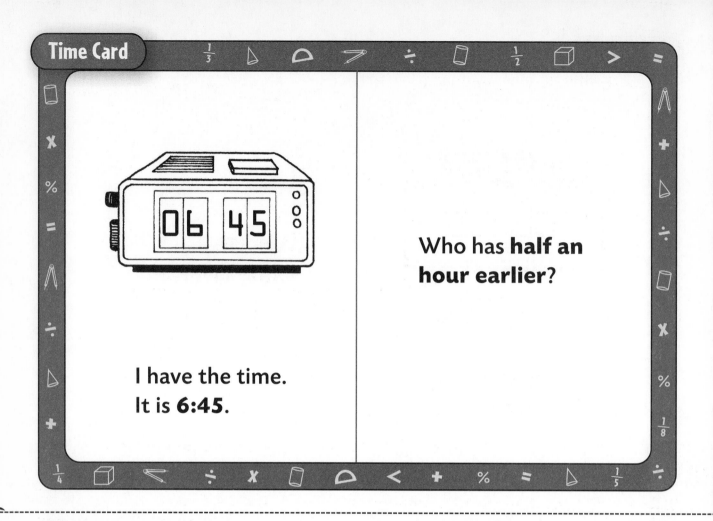

I have the time.
It is **6:45**.

Who has **half an hour earlier?**

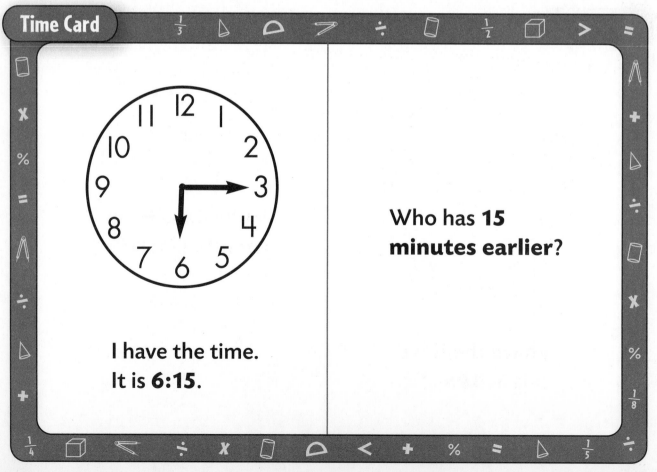

I have the time.
It is **6:15**.

Who has **15 minutes earlier?**

Ask & Answer Interactive Math Practice: Grades 4–6 ©2007 by Joseph A. Porzio, Scholastic Teaching Resources

Time Card

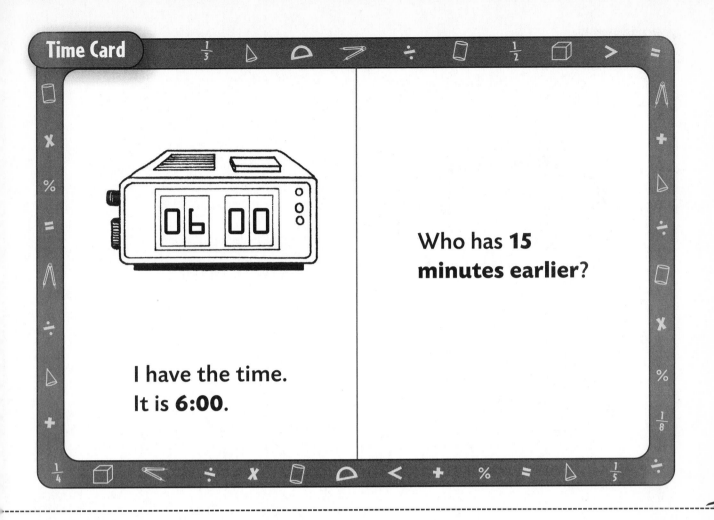

I have the time.
It is **6:00**.

Who has **15 minutes earlier**?

Time Card

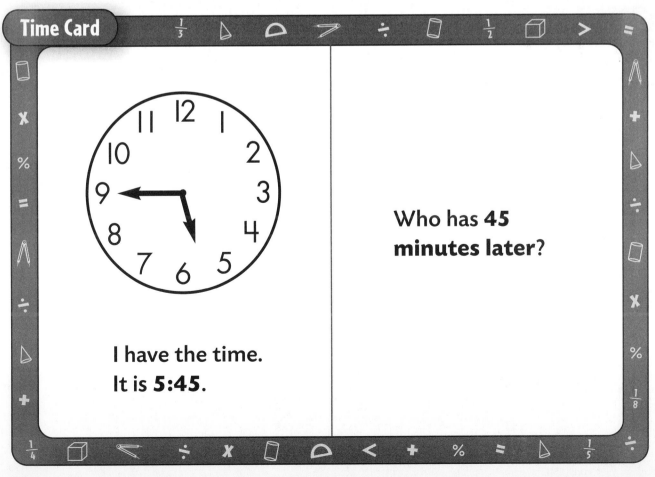

I have the time.
It is **5:45**.

Who has **45 minutes later**?

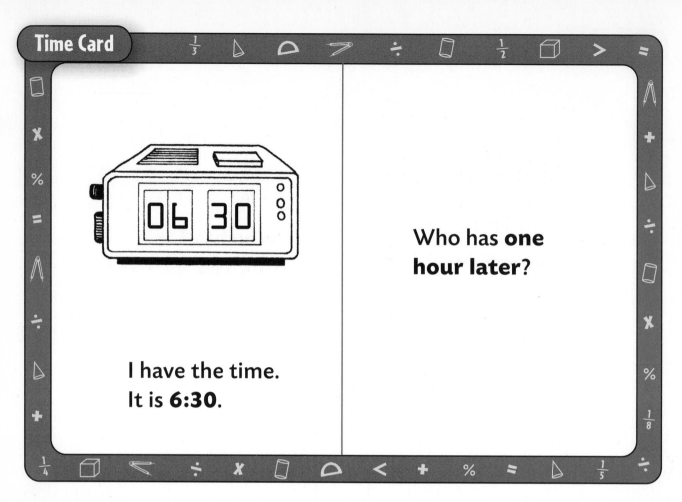

I have the time.
It is **6:30**.

Who has **one hour later?**

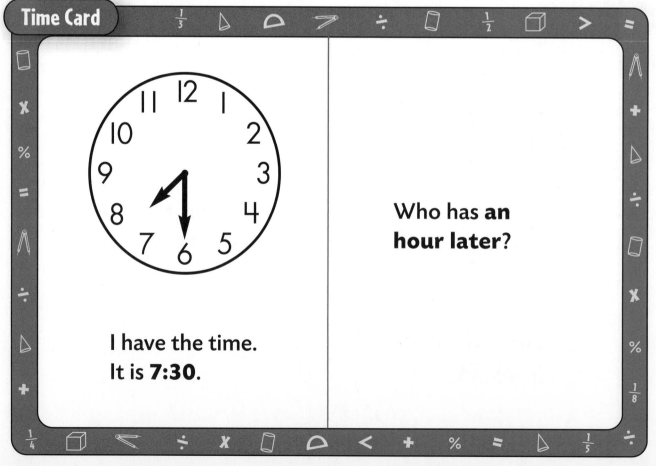

I have the time.
It is **7:30**.

Who has **an hour later?**

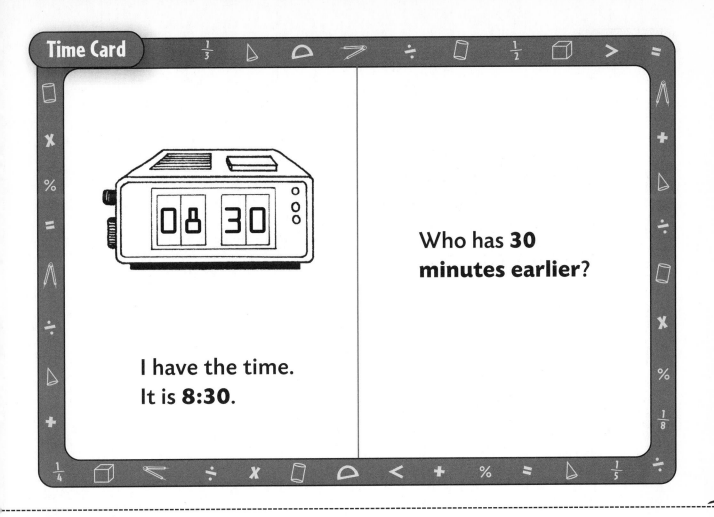

I have the time.
It is **8:30**.

Who has **30 minutes earlier**?

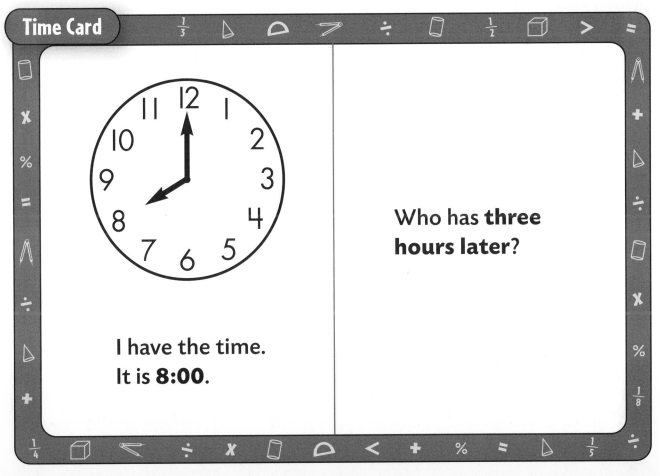

I have the time.
It is **8:00**.

Who has **three hours later**?

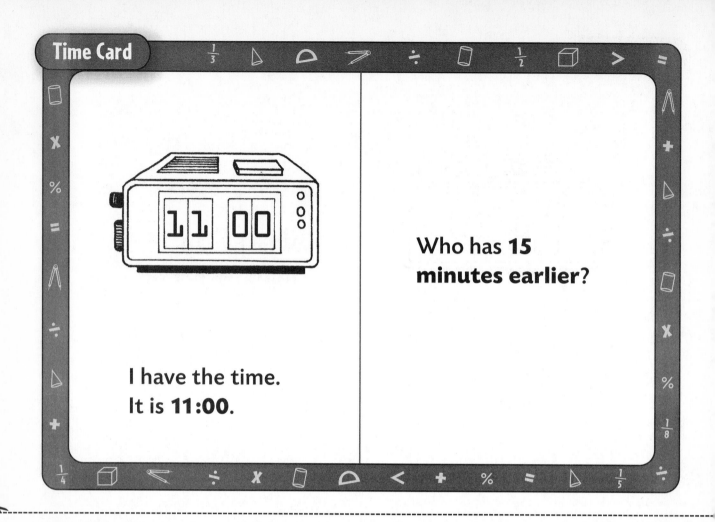

Who has **15 minutes earlier?**

I have the time.
It is **11:00**.

Who has **half an hour earlier?**

I have the time.
It is **10:45**.

Ask & Answer Interactive Math Practice: Grades 4–6 ©2007 by Joseph A. Porzio, Scholastic Teaching Resources

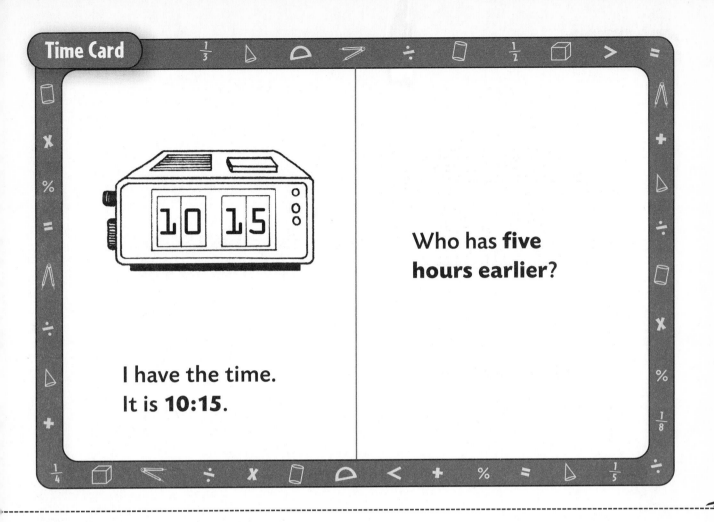

I have the time.
It is **10:15**.

Who has **five
hours earlier**?

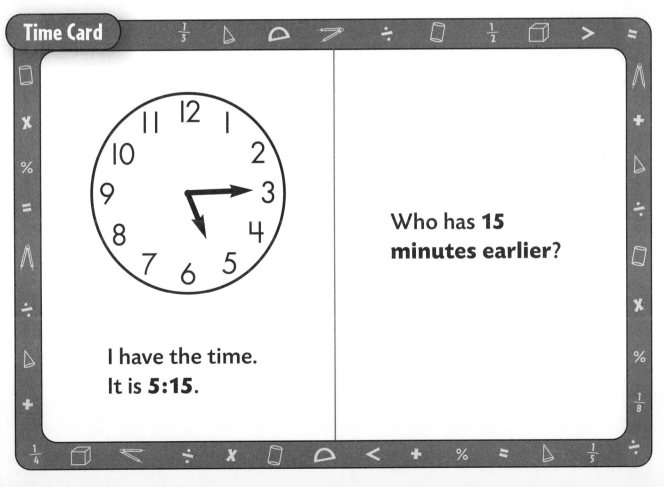

I have the time.
It is **5:15**.

Who has **15
minutes earlier**?

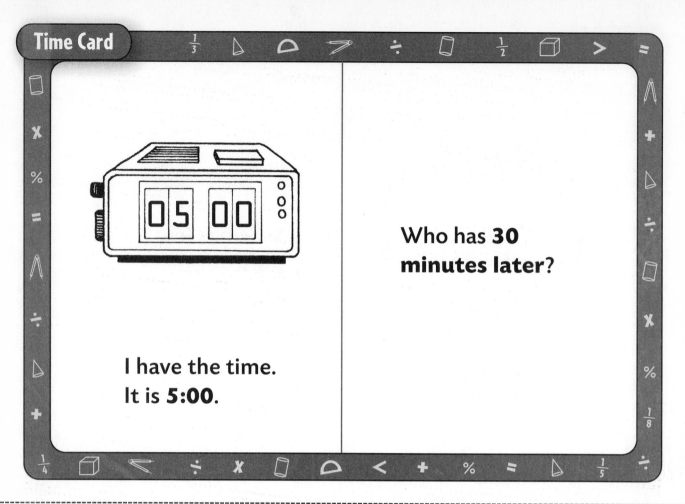

I have the time.
It is **5:00**.

Who has **30 minutes later?**

I have the time.
It is **5:30**.

Who has **four hours later?**

Ask & Answer Interactive Math Practice: Grades 4–6 ©2007 by Joseph A. Porzio, Scholastic Teaching Resources

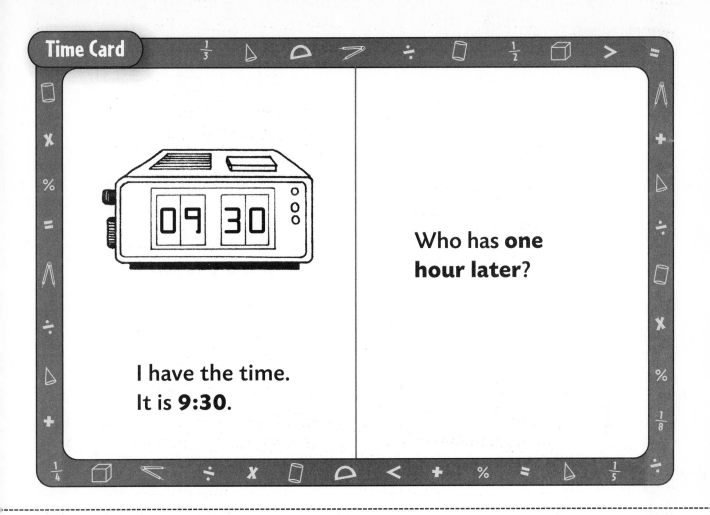

Time Card

I have the time.
It is **9:30**.

Who has **one hour later**?

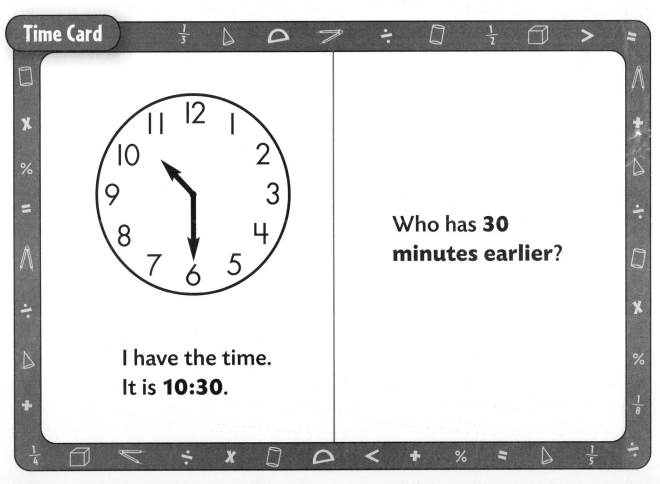

Time Card

I have the time.
It is **10:30**.

Who has **30 minutes earlier**?

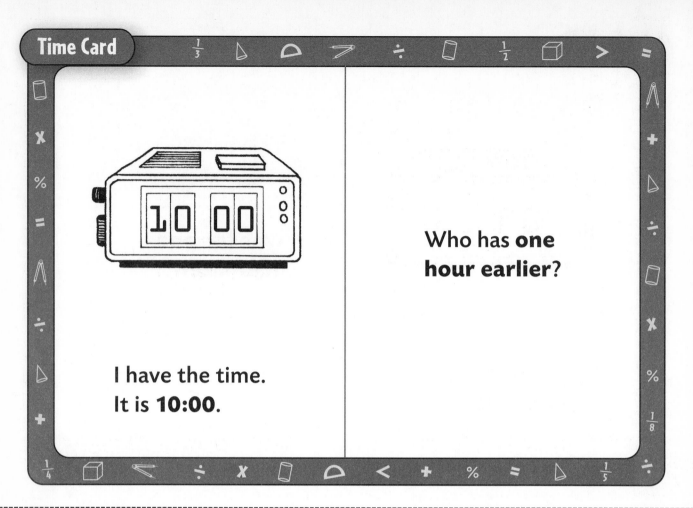

I have the time.
It is **10:00**.

Who has **one hour earlier**?

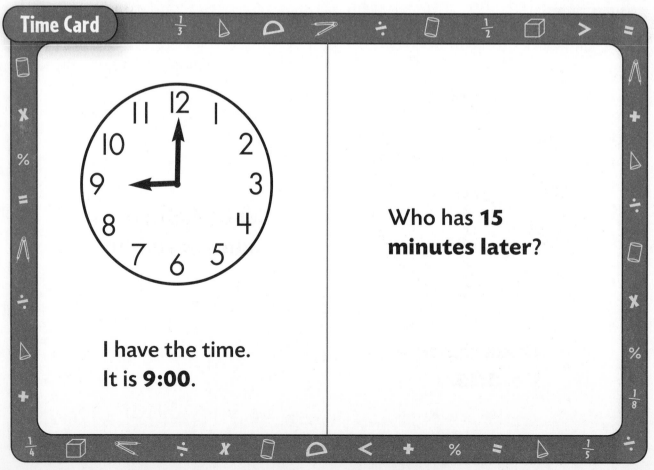

I have the time.
It is **9:00**.

Who has **15 minutes later**?

Ask & Answer Interactive Math Practice: Grades 4-6 ©2007 by Joseph A. Porzio, Scholastic Teaching Resources

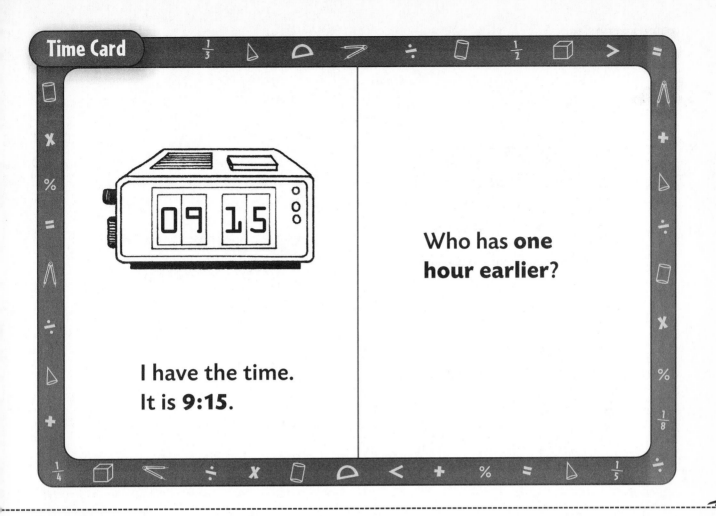

I have the time.
It is **9:15**.

Who has **one hour earlier?**

Ask & Answer Interactive Math Practice: Grades 4–6 ©2007 by Joseph A. Porzio, Scholastic Teaching Resources

Time Card

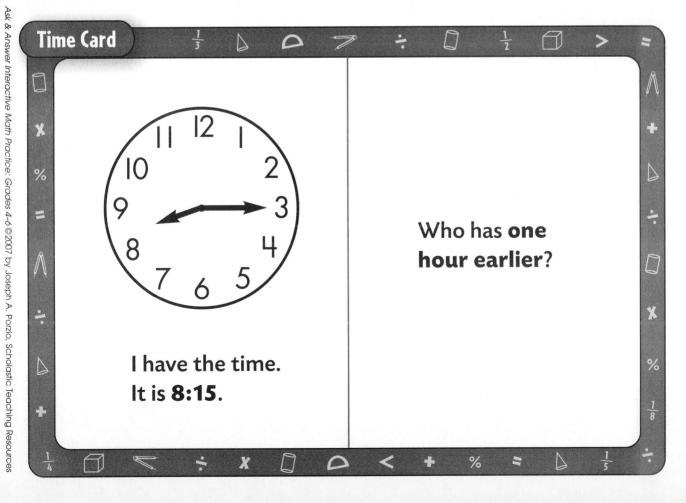

I have the time.
It is **8:15**.

Who has **one hour earlier?**

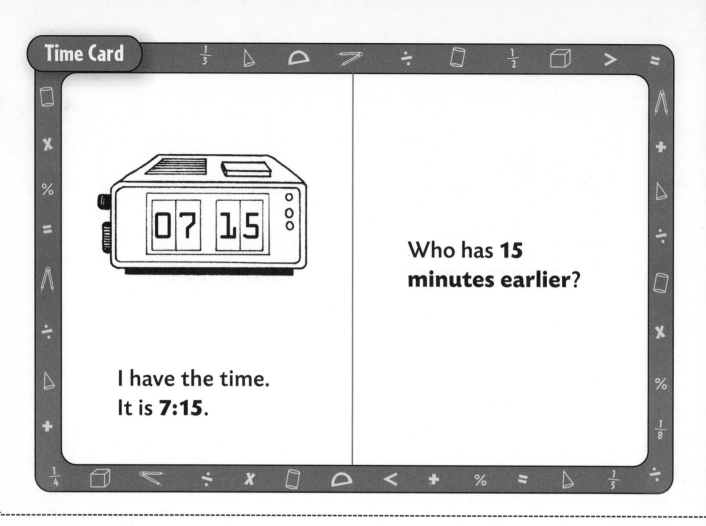

Who has **15 minutes earlier**?

I have the time.
It is **7:15**.

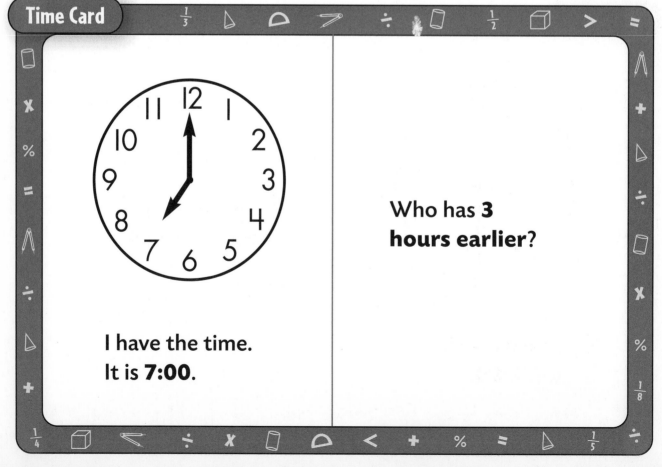

Who has **3 hours earlier**?

I have the time.
It is **7:00**.

Ask & Answer Interactive Math Practice: Grades 4–6 ©2007 by Joseph A. Porzio, Scholastic Teaching Resources

Time Card

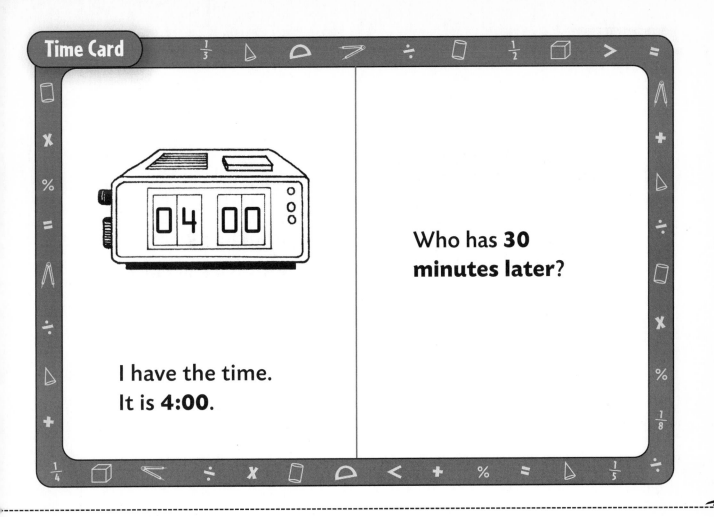

I have the time.
It is **4:00**.

Who has **30 minutes later**?

Time Card

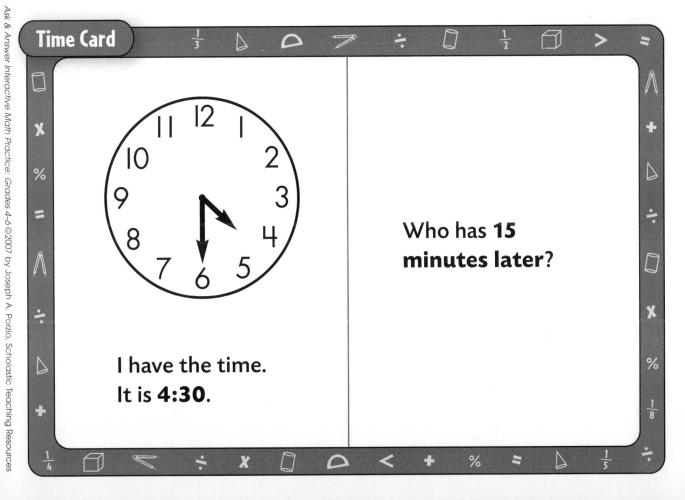

I have the time.
It is **4:30**.

Who has **15 minutes later**?

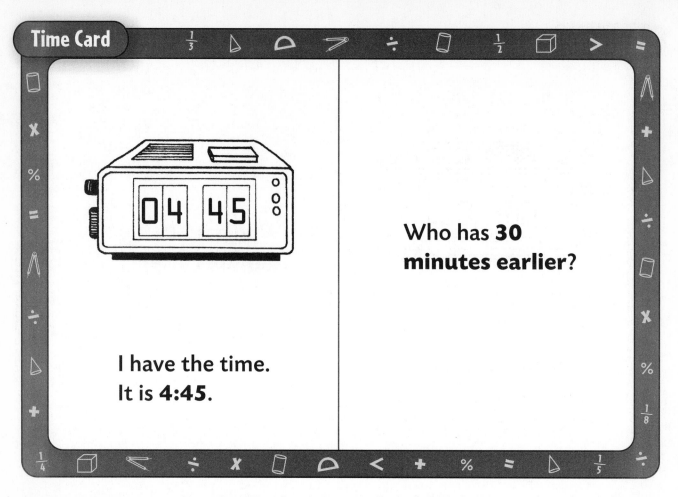

I have the time.
It is **4:45**.

Who has **30 minutes earlier**?

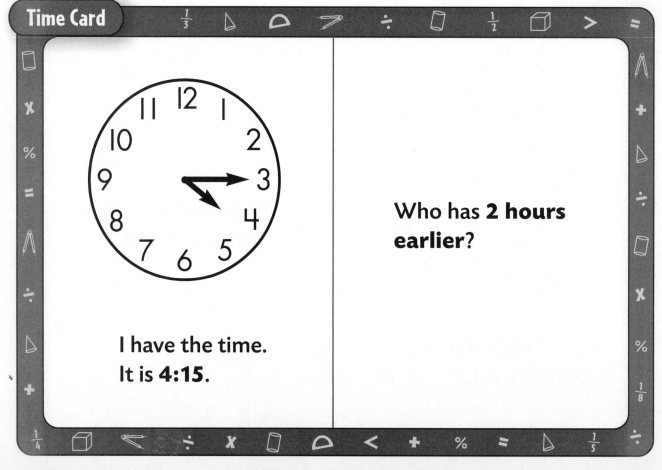

I have the time.
It is **4:15**.

Who has **2 hours earlier**?

Ask & Answer Interactive Math Practice: Grades 4–6 ©2007 by Joseph A. Porzio, Scholastic Teaching Resources

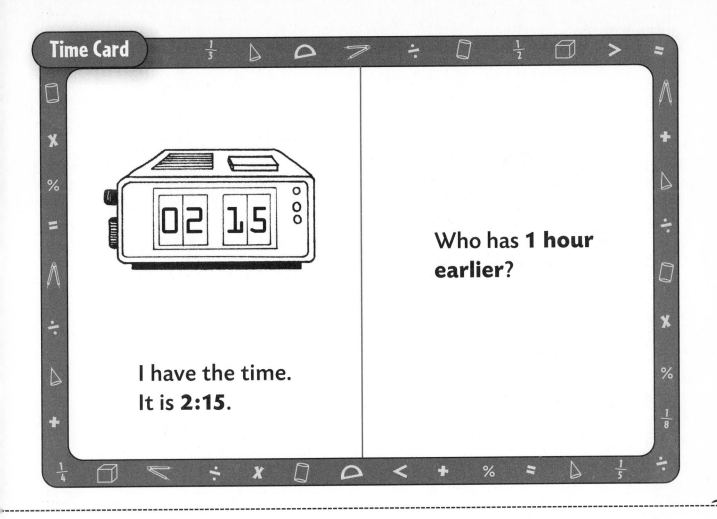

I have the time.
It is **2:15**.

Who has **1 hour earlier?**

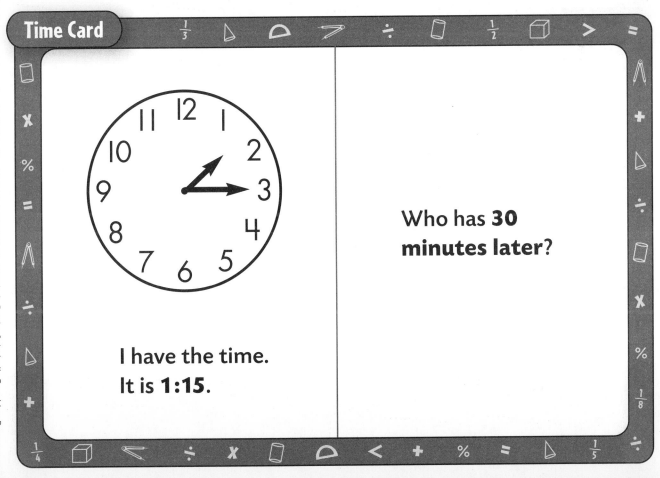

I have the time.
It is **1:15**.

Who has **30 minutes later?**

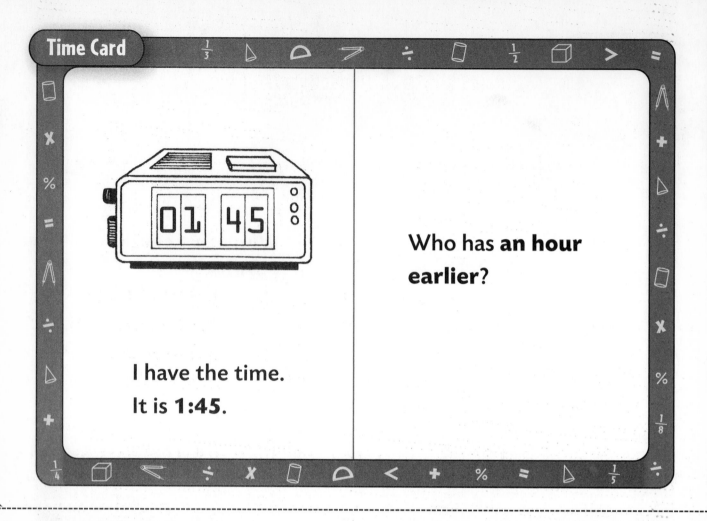

I have the time.
It is **1:45**.

Who has **an hour earlier**?

I have the time.
It is **12:45**.

And now we're out of time!